East of Flatbush, North of Love

An Ethnography of Home

Danielle Brown, Ph.D.

MY PEOPLE TELL STORIES

My People Tell Stories, LLC
New Orleans, LA 70125

Books may be purchased at the publisher's website:
www.mypeopletellstories.com

Consulting Editor: Lea Downing
Interior Design: Heather Michael
Cover Design: Roxanna Allen

ISBN: 978-0-9968443-1-4

Library of Congress Control Number: 2015916692

Printed in the United States of America

To my parents—
In honor of the stories they've told
and the ones they have yet to tell…

Contents

Preface

Wind up the tango-box: "My foot, the wise one, this time said: 'Could you please try to decolonize yourself?'" The tango-box winds down. I wonder, why would you follow me through these pages? I know you did not expect me to address you like this. What kind of introduction is this? I can already sense some restlessness. I lower my voice and answer slowly: i'm ... trying ... to ... decolonize ... myself. I am tempted to apologize, to erase the whole thing and start all over again. Sorry for putting you in the spot, in my point, in the dot, in these stains. An introduction should go like this...

—Marta Savigliano, *Tango and the Political Economy of Passion*[1]

In 2014, after having spent the better part of twelve years in academia, I quietly resigned my position as an Assistant Professor of Music History and Cultures at Syracuse University. I had been living in Syracuse for two years, and the city did not seem conducive to the psychological well-being of a young black woman with no familial ties to the place. My dissatisfaction with the city was perhaps only surpassed by my dissatisfaction with my academic field—ethnomusicology—in particular and, to a certain extent, academia as a whole. The musicological canon was still overly Eurocentric, even in my field where "non-Western" people historically have been overrepresented as subjects (and objects) of study.

---

[1] Marta Savigliano, *Tango and the Political Economy of Passion* (Boulder: Westview Press, 1995), 1.

And perhaps worse, these subjects have been overwhelmingly researched and represented by researchers from outside of their culture. As a minority researcher, I saw little that validated my forms of knowledge, my experiences, my ways of being. I had become disillusioned with the system, and I could feel fatigue setting in. Academia had become a game that I no longer wanted to play, at least not under the current terms. It was time for me to go.

And so, I moved to New Orleans and started a small publishing and production company called My People Tell Stories, LLC. After all, my most significant education had come through the stories that I had learned growing up. And I noticed that in my classes students most connected with material that had a personal component to it—one that allowed them to think about the world of another and simultaneously reflect on their own. Consequently, for the company's first publication, I set out to write a retelling of my dissertation research on parang music in Trinidad. However, the book had other ideas.

"Follow the yellow brick road" was my mother's suggestion to me when I told her that the book kept morphing. I heeded her advice and decided to see where this literary journey would take me. Then, on a rather unassuming day, while visiting home and running errands with my mom in Brooklyn, I thought to myself, "Ethnographic memoir—that's the type of story that I'm writing." However, this was not the kind of ethnographic memoir that involved "non-native" researchers writing reflexive pieces about their fieldwork in a culturally foreign land. As stated in the book's title, this was an "ethnography of home," a story written from a place of familiarity, about places that were crucial to my development during my formative years.

As I began doing some research on ethnographic memoirs, I came across a scholar by the name of Sw. Anand Prahlad, who wrote an article in the *Journal of American Folklore* about his pending project *Getting Happy: An Ethnographic Memoir*. Although it appears that the book was never completed, much of what Prahlad states in his article resonated with me. Prahlad's decision to write an ethnographic memoir was "driven by personal crises arising from the schizophrenia so common among first-generation and minority academicians."[2]

> As many have noted, this fragmentation of self results from spending so many waking hours in an environment hostile to one's most authentic being: an environment in which the Eurocentric, imperialist Mind stands guard over the bees of the hive with a cruel intensity equal to that of plantation overseers. In this case, though, control is enforced through polite, intellectual means rather than through the physical, a kind of control in which the class, race, and personal aesthetics and sensibilities of the institution clash so profoundly with one's own that a resulting psychological quandary is inevitable. This project reflects an effort to recover the parts of myself scattered about like bloody bodies on a field of war after a battle, to nourish them back to health, and to reintegrate them into a whole based not on imperatives handed down by societal institutions, but on that disclaimed shadow that haunts the halls of Western power—the inner, spiritual voice.[3]

In relatively few words, Prahlad aptly captures the reasons for my departure from academia and my decision to write an ethnographic memoir. To say that writing this book served as a sort of therapy for me would be an understatement. Yet, it was not the kind of project that allowed me to effortlessly abandon the norms of the discipline in which I had been enmeshed for several years. I fought myself the

[2] Sw. Anand Prahlad, "Getting Happy: An Ethnographic Memoir," *Journal of American Folklore* 118, no. 467 (2005): 21.

[3] Ibid.

entire way. I was (and still am) fighting an ideology of colonialism and imperialism that is so entrenched in our culture (and really, across the globe) that it is not easily discarded. At times, one has to be hyper-vigilant to detect its presence. Through this project, I was trying to retrieve myself from years of Western education that threatened to promote cultural amnesia. I was trying to decolonize myself before there was nothing left to colonize. There was an urgency to complete this project that was rooted in a certain terror that one feels when one's very existence is threatened. I had to prove (to myself) that I exist, and not because someone else had given me permission to exist.

East of Flatbush, North of Love is a labor of love, an ode to my family and to my culture. My story is neither highly theoretical, nor groundbreaking. It is a simple story of growing up in the West Indian enclave of East Flatbush, Brooklyn. This is not to say that there isn't a serious element that runs throughout. For all its simplicity, it is nonetheless a form of protest. By rejecting conventional ways of writing, I seek to reject conventional ways of thinking. The book calls into question how knowledge is produced and whose knowledge is privileged. Most importantly, it is a way to acknowledge that my people's stories are just as valid as the stories that others tell about us. This is a project about reclaiming power, dignity, and humanity.

I wrote this book not only for myself, but also for young people and adults who, like me, want to see their reflections in the pages that they read, and who are looking to learn a bit more about themselves and their heritage. I also wrote this book for people who know very little about West Indian culture, and, as a result, my teacher persona has guided much of this writing. I have done my best to deliver a story that I hope will foster critical thinking and not merely the absorption of information. And I hope too that my experiences will be used as a safe avenue to talk about topics that make many of us feel uncomfortable, e.g., colonialism, racism, colorism, etc. I share my story because I whole-heartedly believe that unless we exchange our own personal stories, we cannot see where our personal understandings are perhaps shortsighted, unevolved, too localized, or just plain wrong.

As I was writing this book, the deeply rooted racial anxieties and mistrust that had been long simmering just beneath the surface of the American consciousness seemed to have boiled over. And so fostering cross-cultural understanding took on a new urgency. This one book is not meant to transform the world. However, through it I am taking responsibility for myself and doing what my spirit tells me needs to be done. I don't expect to topple the whole system of injustices with this book, but I will remove my support beam, or at least a portion of it.

Danielle Brown
New Orleans, LA
Thursday, August 13, 2015

Notes on How to Use this Book

Language

In the telling of my story, I use a combination of Standard English and Trinidad Creole (or Trinidad English). For the most part, I let the words flow naturally onto the page with little conscious effort to employ one style over the other. I think this practice prevented me from getting too caught up on language; it also reflects the level of comfort that people of West Indian descent feel using both language systems.

With that said, I used phonetic spellings mostly for dialogue. Again, there were no hard and fast rules, primarily because readers who are familiar with certain accents—for example, from New York or Trinidad—usually can "hear" those accents even when standard spellings are employed. Thus, writing phonetically when using Trinidad Creole is not entirely necessary. However, spelling phonetically can help those who are less familiar with particular accents to better "hear" the dialogue. It also serves to lessen the privileging of Standard English over creolized versions, and as such I certainly did not censor it in my writings.

Finally, for those of you who cannot accurately hear a West Indian accent in your head, please don't try to produce one out loud in public without the requisite training. We are sensitive to caricatures. Besides, it usually just sounds bad.

Music and Transcriptions

This book contains, if you will, a music soundtrack. Interspersed throughout, I have listed the names of various songs, along with the appropriate performing artists. These "playlists" serve mainly to set the mood for the sections that follow. The reader is provided with "cues" regarding when to listen to each song, and I encourage you to pay heed to these cues, as it will lead to a more rewarding understanding and interpretation of the material. Most of the songs mentioned are easily accessible and available for purchase online.

Also, unless otherwise noted, all transcriptions and translations are my own. I apologize for any and all lapses in hearing and/or musical taste.

Guidebook[1]

As an educator, I could not help but create a guidebook to accompany this text. The guidebook was designed with the classroom teacher in mind but inspired by the conversations and debates that were commonplace in my family. A range of topics is explored, from map reading and analyzing historical documents, to suggestions on ways to incorporate important but sensitive topics into classroom discussions. In the guidebook, you will find additional reading and listening materials, lesson plans, as well as classroom exercises and assignments. In its entirety, the guidebook is designed to foster critical thinking and prepare students, young and old, to become global citizens.

[1] The guidebook to *East of Flatbush, North of Love* comes under a separate cover; it is not a part of this book.

List of Cued Songs in Order of Appearance

Chapter 1: One Family—East Flatbush

1. "Pretty Boy," *Prophet Benjamin*
2. "Sak Pase," *Krosfyah*
3. "Family," *Lord Nelson*
4. "Empire State of Mind," *Jay Z feat. Alicia Keys*
5. "Ah Home," *Iwer George*
6. "Display," *Fay-Ann Lyons*
7. "Hot, Hot, Hot," *Arrow*
8. "Show It Off," *Beres Hammond*
9. "Gonna Talk," *Beres Hammond*
10. "Murder She Wrote," *Chaka Demus and Pliers*
11. "Bam Bam," *Chaka Demus and Pliers*
12. "Fresh Vegetable," *Tony Rebel*
13. "Tempted to Touch," *Beres Hammond*
14. "Trying to Get to You," *Richie Stephens*
15. "My Adidas," *Run DMC*

Chapter 2: There's No Place Like Home

1. "Back in the Day," *Ahmad*
2. "Kung Fu Fighting," *Carl Douglas*
3. "I Wish," *Stevie Wonder*
4. "Drink Ah Rum," *Lord Kitchener*
5. "Christmas Time," *Salsoul Orchestra*
6. "The Chipmunk Song," *The Chipmunks*
7. "Christmas Won't Be The Same This Year," *The Jackson 5*

8. "Silent Night," *The Temptations*
9. "Trinidad Paseo," *Lovey's String Band*
10. "Sugar Bum Bum," *Lord Kitchener*
11. "The Message," *Grandmaster Flash and the Furious Five*
12. "Ladies First," *Queen Latifah feat. Monie Love*
13. "You Got What I Need," *Biz Markie*
14. "She Keeps on Passin' Me By," *Pharcyde*
15. "Around the Way Girl," *L.L. Cool J*
16. "I Got a Man," *Positive K*
17. "I Used to Lover H.E.R.," *Common Sense (a.k.a. Common)*
18. "Tennessee," *Arrested Development*
19. "You're All I Need," *Marvin Gaye and Tammi Terrell*
20. "Let's Stay Together," *Al Green*
21. "Precious Lord," *Aretha Franklin*
22. "Hold My Mule," *Shirley Caesar*
23. "God's Got It," *Milton Brunson & the Thompson Community Singers*
24. "Tomorrow," *The Winans*
25. "Tiney Winey," *Byron Lee and the Dragonaires*

Chapter 3: Island in the Sun

1. "Island in the Sun," *Harry Belafonte*
2. "Portrait of Trinidad," *Mighty Sniper*
3. "Historia de Trinidad," *San Jose Serenaders*
4. "Federation," *Mighty Sparrow*
5. "Our Model Nation," *Mighty Sparrow*
6. "Mangoes," *Trinidad Folksong*
7. "Trinidad the Godfather," *King Swallow*
8. "Take Yuh Meat Out Muh Rice," *Lord Kitchener*
9. "Kaka Roach," *Lord Kitchener*
10. "Rainorama," *Lord Kitchener*
11. "When Ah Dead Bury Meh Clothes," *Growling Tiger*
12. "Stick Fight," *Anslem Douglas*
13. "Mastife," *David Rudder*
14. "Calypso," *David Rudder*
15. "De Trini Way," *Destra Garcia*
16. "Dead or Alive," *Shurwayne Winchester*
17. "The Road," *Lord Kitchener*
18. "Outcast," *Mighty Sparrow*

19. "Pan in 'A' Minor," *Lord Kitchener*
20. "Pan in 'A' Minor," *Renegades Steel Orchestra*
21. "The Hammer," *David Rudder*
22. "Calling Meh," *Destra Garcia*
23. "The Grinch," *Myron B*
24. "Caminante," *Baron*
25. "Sereno, sereno," *La Divina Pastora*
26. "A la medianoche," *La Divina Pastora*
27. "Alegría," *La Divina Pastora*
28. "Good Mornin," *3 Canal*

Chapter 4: Of God, Ghosts, and Obeah

1. "Lorraine," *Explainer*
2. "Karele, Karele O (Oshun Karele)," *Ella Andall*
3. "Ogun Ye Ku De Ye Baba," *Ella Andall*
4. "Shango," *Roaring Lion*
5. "Caribbean Medley," *Donnie McClurkin*
6. "The Prayers," *J. Moss*
7. "Faith," *Kirk Franklin's Nu Nation*
8. "My God, My God, My God," *Sandra Crouch*
9. "Completely Yes," *Sandra Crouch*
10. "Take Me Back," *Andraé Crouch*
11. "Soon and Very Soon," *Andraé Crouch*
12. "Break Every Chain," *Tasha Cobbs*
13. "Love in the Cemetery," *Lord Kitchener*
14. "Obeah Wedding," *Mighty Sparrow*
15. "Yerbero moderno," *Celia Cruz*
16. "Jumbie," *Scrunter*

Chapter 5: The Empire Strikes

1. "Rum and Coca-Cola," *Andrews Sisters*
2. "Rum and Coca-Cola," *Lord Invader*
3. "Yankee Dollar," *Lord Invader*
4. "Jean and Dinah," *Mighty Sparrow*
5. "Boom Up History," *3 Canal*

6. "Talk Yuh Talk," *3 Canal*
7. "Slave," *Mighty Sparrow*
8. "Say It Loud—I'm Black and I'm Proud," *James Brown*
9. "Black is Beautiful," *Mighty Duke*
10. "Split Me in Two," *Mighty Dougla*
11. "African," *Brother Superior*
12. "I Am Not My Hair," *India Arie*
13. "Four Women," *Nina Simone*
14. "¿Y tu abuela a'onde e'tá?" *Luis Carbonell*
15. "Negro bembón," *Ismael Rivera*

Chapter 6: An Immigrant in My Own Land

1. "Doing Time," *Roderick Gordon*
2. "Nah Leaving," *Denyse Plummer*
3. "Trini 2 De Bone," *David Rudder w/Carl Jacobs*
4. "The Hood Ain't the Same," *Draze*
5. "Inner City Blues," *Marvin Gaye*
6. "Family," *Lord Nelson*

Chapter 1: One Family—East Flatbush

Mom always says you should be proud of where you're from. Because of this, I never liked when I'd ask some one where they're from and they would say, "A little town outside of [enter some major city]." How is anyone going to know that your little town exists, that your people exist, if you don't put it and them on the map?
—Me

Cue: "Pretty Boy," Prophet Benjamin

"Yuh hair look just like my own," he said, approaching me as I waited impatiently for the B44 to arrive. The other bodies at the bus stop appeared content in their boredom, but this gentleman could not let the time pass without bugging some unsuspecting soul—me—for a bit of conversation.

I looked at his long, un-stylized, matted locks. He had some *real* Rastaman dreads, *boi*. He was well over six feet and his locks hung past his waist. He must have been growing them for a long time, because the ends—some of which were on the verge of dropping off—were a shade of brown far removed from the gray roots that sprung from his scalp. I had to chuckle. His hair was a far cry from the two-stranded twists that adorned my head. Granted, there was nothing fancy about my hairdo. (I was on my way to teach a piano lesson, not a wedding.) Yet, I couldn't help but think to myself, "My hair does *not* look like yours."

I don't remember what I actually said to him, but it was something more polite. He then asked, "Trini?"

"Yeah. Born here, but Trini background. How yuh know?"

"Ah could hear it when yuh talk."

He wasn't Trini, but I couldn't quite place the accent. Them small island accents can be tricky. Before I could ask him where he was from, the bus pulled up to the corner. We weren't in a hurry to get on, so we let the more impatient ones make their way to the front of the bus. By the time we had gotten on, there weren't any more seats, so we continued our conversation standing amongst the other Caribbean bodies on board.

As he towered over my five foot four inch frame, he told me he was from Grenada but that he had lived in Trinidad for several years, so he was quite adept at picking up a Trini accent. Honestly, I don't remember much else about that conversation, but we continued making chit-chat until he got off of the bus a few minutes later. I stayed on. I was going all the way to Bushwick.

Bushwick was a long pull from where I'd begun my encounter with the Grenadian Rastaman. We'd met at the corner of New York Avenue and Avenue D in East Flatbush—a Caribbean outpost, literally in the middle of Brooklyn. Growing up, people here were mostly from various parts of the English-speaking Caribbean. Like Rastaman so astutely ascertained, my family is from the twin-island Republic of Trinidad and Tobago, but others—like him—hail from elsewhere in the Caribbean, including Jamaica, Barbados, St. Vincent, and Grenada. There are folks from the mainland, too—immigrants from Guyana, and some Central Americans, primarily from Panama. If you live here, and you're not a first or second-generation immigrant, you're an anomaly.

As its name suggests, East Flatbush is a neighborhood in Brooklyn that is situated east of Flatbush Avenue, a main thoroughfare in Brooklyn, and an important street in this ethnic enclave. Flatbush Avenue, like the other major roads that flow through East Flatbush—Church Avenue, Utica Avenue, Nostrand Avenue—are teeming with a wide array of businesses all catering primarily to the neighborhood's Caribbean population.

To be more precise, we are West Indians—people from the West Indies, so-called because Christopher Columbus got lost on his way to India. We are people who share a history and culture rooted in the forced migration, enslavement, and indentured servitude of indigenous, African, and Asian bodies.[1] Although technically the West Indies consists of the entire Caribbean basin, and includes the British, French, Spanish, and Dutch West Indies, the term "West Indian" is used in very specific ways. In general, West Indians are people who by virtue of birth or descent are from the original thirteen member states of the Caribbean Community and Common Market (CARICOM).[2] This includes people from Guyana on the South American continent and Belize (formerly British Honduras) in Central America. Although Panama is not a member of CARICOM, a significant number of Panamanians are descendants of West Indian migrants, many of whom went to Panama to work on the building of its famed canal. I certainly include them as part of the West Indian community in East Flatbush. And while there may be other Central Americans of West Indian descent living in East Flatbush, Panamanians are

[1] By and large, West Indians are descendants of enslaved Africans who arrived in the Caribbean as part of the Trans-Atlantic Slave Trade. However, places like Guyana and Trinidad have large numbers of ethnic East Indians who came to the region as indentured servants. Smaller numbers of ethnic Chinese, Syrians, Lebanese, and Europeans are also present on some islands, like Trinidad and Jamaica.

[2] Antigua and Barbuda, the Bahamas, Barbados, Belize (formerly British Honduras), Dominica, Grenada, Guyana, Jamaica, Montserrat, St. Kitts-Nevis-Anguilla, St. Lucia, St. Vincent and the Grenadines, and Trinidad and Tobago. Caribbean Community Secretariat, "History of the Caribbean Community (CARICOM)," *caricom.org*, accessed August 16, 2015, http://www.caricom.org/jsp/community/history.jsp?menu=community.

by far the most recognizable group,[3] as evident by the number of Panamanian flags that can be seen throughout the neighborhood.

Cue: "Sak Pase," Krosfyah

Living side by side with West Indians are people from other parts of the Caribbean.[4] In particular, East Flatbush has a large Haitian population that cannot be ignored. Their presence has been an important part of my growing up in East Flatbush, and their numbers and influence in the community have only increased over the years, particularly since the devastating earthquake that hit Haiti in 2010. But in the 1980s, Haitians weren't too proud to be called Haitian. In school, kids would make fun of them, claiming they were poor, dirty, and unkempt. The association of Haitians with "voodoo," and the negative perceptions that went along with that, only added to their ostracization. The situation was so bad that some would try to deny their heritage, claiming, for instance, to be Jamaican or Trinidadian instead. My mom, an educator, once had to tell a junior high school student not to lie about being Haitian.

"You must be proud of where you're from," she told him.

In those days, it was rare to hear Haitian Kreyòl spoken on the streets, especially by young people. One could only imagine that they must have hoped that the language would forever release its hold on their tongues.

Things began to change in the 1990s and early 2000s. Haitian pride began to take effect publically as Haitians mobilized

---

[3] From the late 19th century until the first few decades of the 20th, a significant number of West Indians migrated to other parts of Central America, including Costa Rica and Honduras, seeking employment. Many found work on the "banana plantations" in those countries. As a result, those nations are also home to a significant number of people of West Indian descent.

[4] I use the term West Indian to refer to people who are from those thirteen original CARICOM states. The term Caribbean is used in reference to people from the general Caribbean region and circum-Caribbean.

in reaction to political unrest in their homeland,[5] as well as police brutality in New York City. The case of Abner Louima, a security guard, who, while in police custody, was brutally beaten and sodomized with a foreign object[6] by some depraved members of the NYPD, seemed to me to be a turning point.

I was shocked the first time I heard young people speaking Kreyòl on the streets. I can't remember exactly when it happened, but it was probably sometime during the first few years of the new millennium. There they were, some young girls of Haitian descent; they were loud and spoke unabashedly. It seemed like everywhere I turned, there were more like them. I'm not Haitian, but I was proud.

Cue: "Family," Lord Nelson

Thankfully, the perception of Haitians (and their self-perception) has changed over the years, but within the West Indian community people have always held certain beliefs regarding the characteristics of each island's citizens. Trinis are the fun-loving ones of the bunch. "They too happy," as my mother would say. They are also known as the tricksters of the group, playfully (or pejoratively) referred to as "Trickidadians." Bajans are perceived as more educated, proper, and serious. Jamaicans are the ones who are most well known internationally, in no small part because of Bob Marley, but in East Flatbush, they are one of us. If I had to place them in a yearbook category, I might vote Jamaicans as the most likely to get into a fight. However, it's hard to generalize too much, because within each island there are regional differences, as well as those based on socio-economic class, education, and religion, among others. But whatever our differences, it doesn't preclude us from getting along.

In her study of the West Indian community in Brooklyn, Mary Waters interviewed immigrants and asked them to de-

---

[5] Haitians living in New York City protested the 1991 coup d'état, which ousted newly elected president, Jean-Bertrand Aristide.

[6] The object was the broken handle of a broom or plunger.

scribe their perceptions of people from the different West Indian islands. She states:

> What is striking in the patterns of responses is that respondents could describe various cultural differences across the islands, but these perceived differences did not seem to affect the respondents' willingness to be grouped together as West Indians or to affect their attitudes toward very close interactions such as intermarriage.[7]

Like siblings, we may fight and "bad talk" each other every now and again, but it doesn't change the fact that "all ah we is one family," especially in New York City.[8]

Cue: "Empire State of Mind," Jay Z feat. Alicia Keys

Although just five percent of immigrants in the U.S. are classified as "non-Hispanic Caribbean," this group (which includes West Indians) accounts for roughly twenty percent of the foreign-born population in New York City.[9] New York has the second-highest foreign-born population in the country,[10] most of it concentrated in New York City, which is arguably

---

[7] Mary C. Waters, *Black Identities: West Indian Immigrant Dreams and American Realities* (Cambridge: Harvard University Press, 1999), 58.

[8] To my knowledge, in New York City there's never been any significant feud amongst different West Indian nationalities, especially nothing like that which has existed between Puerto Ricans and Dominicans, which can only be described as venomous.

[9] Arun Peter Lobo and Joseph J. Salvo, "The Newest New Yorkers, 2013 Edition" *NYC Planning*, Department of City Planning City of New York, 12, accessed August 16, 2015, http://www.nyc.gov/html/dcp/pdf/census/nny2013/nny_2013.pdf.

[10] Yesenia D. Acosta, G. Patricia de la Cruz, Christine Gambino, Elizabeth M. Grieco, Thomas Gryn, Luke J. Larsen, Edward N. Trevelyan, and Nathan P. Walters, "The Foreign-Born Population in the United States: 2010," *United States Census Bureau,* U.S. Department of Commerce, 4, accessed August 16, 2015, http://www.census.gov/content/dam/Census/library/publications/2012/acs/acs-19.pdf.

the most diverse city in the world.[11] Foreign-born mothers account for fifty-one percent of all births in the city, resulting in approximately sixty percent of New Yorkers being immigrants or the children of immigrants.[12]

As a result of its significant immigrant population, New York is a city that consists of many races and ethnicities, and its neighborhoods have historically been divided along those lines. Harlem, "Little Italy," and Chinatown are areas that are world-renowned for historically being hubs of African American, Italian, and Chinese culture, respectively. East Harlem, or "El Barrio" as it is affectionately called, has been home to generations of Puerto Ricans, and over the past several decades, Washington "Quisqueya" Heights has developed into a center of Dominican culture. These are just a handful of the many ethnic neighborhoods in the city. Each one has its own characteristics, its own flavor, and its own collective sense of unity and pride. You'll know what neighborhood you're in by being observant. The sights, sounds, and smells say it all.

West Indies!
Show meh allyuh hand!
All West Indians,
Show me allyuh flag!
All West Indians,
Caribbean people me say put up allyuh hand!
—"Ah Home," Iwer George

Cue: "Ah Home," Iwer George

"Someone from Trinidad is here," I said, as I collected my ten-year-old self and ran down the stairs to the first floor.

Indeed, not just someone, but two people from Trinidad

[11] Lobo and Salvo, "Newest New Yorkers," 2.

[12] Ibid., 12.

had arrived. I'm still not sure what it was that tipped me off. Perhaps it was the soap or perfume emanating from their skin, or the detergent with which they washed their clothes. Maybe it was the *tulum* and tamarind balls, sesame seed candies and *kurma* that they packed in their bags to give us living "ah foreign" a taste of "home." Regardless, the Caribbean has a smell, and they had brought it with them.

While even the best perfume could hardly capture the smell of the Caribbean's flora and fauna after a rain shower, or the smell of the sea wafting in a breeze, in East Flatbush, the scent of the Caribbean is recreated stateside. It comes from the choking smell of jerk chicken as it's cooked street-side on a pit, or from curry being prepared by a neighbor. It comes from the aroma of hot peppers permeating the air—peppers that flavor foods from throughout the Caribbean, like *escovitch* fish, *pelau*, and *oil down*. Sometimes it's the smell of food, and sometimes it's the smell of household products like Florida Water, Alcolado, and *blue soap* that bring the scent of the Caribbean to East Flatbush. Either way, our culture and our way of life look, sound, smell, and taste like the Caribbean.

Standing on any corner in East Flatbush, one sees various hues of black and brown—men and women, young and old, people of all shapes and sizes. Women are proud of their shapes, no matter how *obzokie*[13] they appear in their ill-fitting clothes. Rastamen, like my Grenadian friend, don heavy locks with pride, their hair flowing freely or tucked up under oversized hats. Other men walk confidently through the streets with twists, braids, low cut trims, and fades. Sisters sport equally diverse hairstyles—dreads, twists, braids, perms,[14] or hair hidden under hats and scarves. These are the faces and bodies that confront me when I step outside of my house.

Some of these bodies move quickly in step with the pace of the city, while others stroll as though on island time. And

---

[13] Trinidadian word meaning misshapen or funny-shaped.

[14] Black women often use the word "perm" to refer to hair that has been chemically straightened or "relaxed."

as they move along the major streets and avenues, people pass and sometimes duck in and out of any number of businesses. There is no shortage of markets selling produce, meat, fish, and West Indian and American goods. Fish markets sell Caribbean favorites like kingfish, redfish, and shark. Inside the neighborhood grocery stores and produce markets, one can purchase many ingredients used in Caribbean cooking—pigtail, oxtail, and pigeon peas; dasheen bush, pumpkin, and curry. Occasionally, especially in the summertime, one can catch street vendors selling mangoes, coconuts, sugarcane, and other tropical foods.

Major fast food chains like Popeye's and McDonald's, as well as small businesses selling Chinese food and fried chicken, share blocks with mom-and-pop eateries that serve Caribbean food. Some of these mom-and-pop stores have become fixtures in the West Indian community in Brooklyn. Along Nostrand Avenue, Allan's Bakery was the place to go for currant rolls, coconut rolls, and hard dough bread. A little further up the avenue, Gloria's—which now has several restaurants—was a must if you wanted a nice roti. But new establishments are always emerging, and some become household names and give good competition to the older venues.

Besides food-based establishments, there are several other businesses that function as the heartbeat of life in East Flatbush and the larger West Indian community in Brooklyn. If there is a need, someone will attempt to provide it. Hardware stores and locksmiths abut clothing, "variety," and "99¢ stores." Hair salons are interspersed amongst *botánicas*,[15] liquor stores, law offices, realtors, travel agencies, nightclubs, and bars. Major banks and cell phone companies also make their presence known. Not all of these businesses are owned and operated by

---

[15] Botánicas are shops that sell paraphernalia for use in various religious and spiritual practices. Typical items found in botánicas include herbs, candles, Florida Water, and a variety of charms. Many of those served by botánicas are involved in neo-African religions developed in the Americas (including Haitian Vodou, Trinidad Orisha, and Cuban Santería) and/or *obeah*, a practice in Trinidad and other parts of the Caribbean that is akin to what some might call "black magic."

West Indians or members of the community, but they all cater to that population.

Scattered amidst these storefront businesses are houses of worship that represent the comingling of African and European sacred traditions in the Caribbean. Catholic and Anglican churches reflect the influence of European religious practices during the colonial period, while the more recent influence of North American missionaries to the Caribbean is evident in the number of Jehovah's Witnesses, as well as Pentecostal and other evangelical denominations present in East Flatbush. Neo-African sacred traditions are less visible, but certainly present as well. They are maintained by Spiritual Baptists and Orisha practitioners (who are sometimes one and the same), as well as by Haitian vodouists. Symbols of Rastafari, notably the Lion of Judah and the red, yellow, and green colors of the Rastafari flag, can be seen throughout the neighborhood and are used by both practitioners and sympathizers of the faith. And if one is observant, one will notice the triangular shaped flags of the Hindu faith protruding out of the front lawns of some homes.

Show me your colors
Put them up in the sky
Let me see everybody
Get something to beautify
—"Display," Fay-Ann Lyons

Cue: "Display," Fay-Ann Lyons

One of the most telling signs that one is in a West Indian neighborhood is the presence of colorful flags, representing almost every West Indian nation. They hang from rearview mirrors and from apartment windows. They hang from the tops of neighborhood grocery stores, symbolizing the people living in the community and their collective pride. People take their flags with them to fêtes, pulling them out of front and back pockets or handbags and knapsacks, depending on the occasion. Growing up living in a West Indian community, as I did, you learn to recognize the flags of the different islands.

But truthfully, you don't even need to walk the streets of New York to know what neighborhood you're in. Just take a ride on the subway, and you'll see what I mean. Flatbush Avenue, Newkirk Avenue, Beverley Road, Church Avenue, Winthrop Street, Sterling Place, President Street, and Franklin Avenue. These are the names of the subway stops along the numbers 2 and 5 trains in Brooklyn that speed their way through Flatbush, East Flatbush, and Crown Heights, connecting West Indian communities in Brooklyn to each other and to communities beyond. At Franklin Avenue, you can catch the downtown numbers 3 and 4 trains, which take riders further into Crown Heights; the 4 train makes a last stop at Utica Avenue, and the 3 train continues burrowing its way into the predominantly African American community of Brownsville.

When I was growing up, as you moved north of Franklin Avenue, the passengers on the train became increasingly white. Then as the trains progressed into Downtown Brooklyn and Manhattan, a wide range of races and ethnicities would emerge before black and brown bodies would again predominate as the train moved further north, beyond the Upper West Side and Upper East Side of Manhattan. Various points along each subway line tell a story, the history of a community, and how and why groups of people built their lives in particular areas.

The hustle and bustle of the city resumes above ground. As you hit the sidewalk you are bombarded with the sounds of traffic. Dollar cabs and dollar vans zoom up and down streets looking for fares, looking for the Almighty American Dollar. You'll likely hear them coming before you even see them.

Beep! Beep! Beep!

"Utica Avenue! One dollar! One dollar!" the drivers shout from the windows of their vehicles.

As their voices ring out, much is potentially revealed about their heritage. Each island has its own unique speech patterns; they are like fingerprints pointing to a specific national identity.

In true New York fashion, I'd generally roll my eyes and act annoyed as taxi drivers approached and incessantly honked their horns as I waited at the bus stop. The only time I wasn't annoyed was when I actually needed a ride. But as much as I may have been annoyed with the aggressive tactics of some drivers, the dollar cabs and vans provided, and still provide, a useful service to the community. To many immigrants, they feel familiar, functioning similarly to modes of transportation on many Caribbean islands.[16] Drivers drive up and down major streets picking up passengers and dropping them off further along the route. Cheaper and faster than the public buses run by the New York Metropolitan Transit Authority, or the MTA as it is commonly called, many people rely on dollar cabs and vans to get to work and other destinations. The service has been vital, especially during MTA strikes and natural disasters.[17]

The last time I got into a dollar cab, it was raining heavily. So, when a cab pulled up to the bus stop where I was waiting, I decided to get in. As I left, I handed the driver a dollar bill, which he graciously accepted. Later that day, I managed to tell my mom and brother about the incident, to which my brother replied, "You know the dollar cab costs $1.25 now?"

Today, these dollar cabs and vans will cost you a cool $2 per ride. Notably, it's still cheaper than riding the MTA buses and trains.[18]

---

[16] In Trinidad, minibuses, known as *maxis* or *maxi-taxis*, function similarly to Brooklyn's dollar vans. The maxis are color-coded, indicating the area of the country (or corridor) that they service. Equivalent forms of transportation are known as *tap-taps* in Haiti and *guaguas* in Puerto Rico and other part of the Spanish-speaking Americas.

[17] Nate Lavey and Aaron Reiss, "New York's Shadow Transit," *The New Yorker*, Condé Nast, accessed August 16, 2015, http://projects.newyorker.com/story/nyc-dollar-vans/.

[18] Currently, the fare for a local bus or subway ride is $2.75 if purchased with a Pay-Per-Ride MetroCard. A SingleRide ticket costs $3.00. For more information, see http://web.mta.info/metrocard/mcgtreng.htm#payper.

Cue: "Hot, Hot, Hot," Arrow[19]

When the weather is warm, West Indian voices permeate the air, and during the late 1980s and early 1990s, a hot summer's night in East Flatbush was bound to find me in bed, restless from the muggy heat in our air-condition-less house and the excessive noise on the street. The sounds of fireworks and firecrackers, the especially loud ones like cherry bombs and M-80s, would rock the block. Blended in were the sounds of dancehall and soca streaming from competing sound systems, the DJs all seemingly trying to determine who could out-fête who. The music never seemed to end, at least not while the sun lay sleeping. It all melded seamlessly with the redundant and unforgettable melody of the Mr. Softee ice cream truck. And as I tossed in my bed, I would get angry—too much heat, too much noise. But then a DJ would play "my song," and my fury would subside until a new, decidedly less hip song was thrown in the mix. I wasn't particularly fond of these late-night shenanigans, but as they became less frequent as the 90s progressed, and increasingly so in the new millennium, I found myself becoming nostalgic for the old days.

The music that blasted from the streets suggested a certain pride. The music represented us as individual people, individual nations, and as a collective body of people who share a common culture and a common experience as immigrants. Calypso, soca, reggae, and dancehall emanated from the streets, infecting homes and bodies, the entire soundscape. The music spoke to us, and we embodied it. I learned how to "wine"[20] at a young age. I'm not sure how, but I suspect it was by osmosis. However, as a child—perhaps no more than five years old—I remember visiting the apartment of my mom's friend, Pearl, who took it upon herself to make sure that I could do the dance.

"Yuh know how tuh wine?" she asked.

---

[19] I have to say, I'm tired of this song; it's been overplayed. But this was the jam back in the day. Big up Montserrat massive!

[20] A dance movement that involves rolling one's waist from side to side or in a circular motion. It can be performed slowly or quickly.

I shook my head in the affirmative.

"Lemme see if yuh could wine."

And with that, we began to roll our waists from side to side, and we had a jolly good time, too. Technically, Pearl didn't live in East Flatbush, as her apartment stood on the other (west) side of Flatbush Avenue, just off the corner of Ocean Avenue and Beverly Road. I'm sure that we visited her apartment on several occasions, but truthfully, I'm not sure exactly how much time we spent with Pearl as I was growing up. Regardless, the day of our "wining session" has always stuck out in my mind, and I think of her every time I happen to be in the vicinity of that apartment where it all took place.

It's been a long time since I've seen Pearl. She used to go "home" every year for Carnival. One year she didn't make it back. She died in a car accident while in Trinidad for the festivities. Every time I take a wine, I take it for Pearl, in the spirit of "freeing up" oneself.

In general, the calypso and soca music that I listened to partially served the purpose of helping people to "free up," to let go of their collective worries and just be in the moment. As such, these musics have been a vital part of carnival celebrations in Trinidad. However, the music served another purpose—to keep us connected to our community and heritage by teaching us history, life lessons, and values. But I'll get to that a little bit later.

Cue: "Show It Off," "Gonna Talk," Beres Hammond; "Murder She Wrote," "Bam Bam," Chaka Demus and Pliers; "Fresh Vegetable," Tony Rebel; "Tempted to Touch," Beres Hammond; "Trying to Get to You," Richie Stephens

Though symbols of Jamaican identity, I still jammed to reggae and dancehall, as did others in my community, irrespective of their backgrounds. It was hard to resist the suave voice of Beres Hammond, who kept it real with his "lovers rock." He had the best *tabanca*[21] songs to get your slow jam on.

[21] Tabanca is a Trini word that refers to the feeling one has when love is gone or unrequited.

He knew how to make young girls and women feel beautiful, while making boys and men look *strupid*[22] for not knowing a good thing until it was gone.

Dancehall was edgier, and it gave us an opportunity to try out different styles of dancing. It seemed like every other week there was a new dance coming out—the tick, Bogle, Santa Barbara, butterfly, and pepper seed. We used to dance all of them. And then I got too old to keep up. The good DJs knew how to mix the music; they moved seamlessly from one song to the next, keeping the dancers happy. They were the ones who could keep my friends and me dancing for hours on the same *riddim*.[23] They were the ones who could induce me to dance in bed, making me forget that I was mad when the thumping of the bass from a too-loud sound system had woken me up in the middle of the night.

All they had to do was play one of them real hot riddims, like the "Murder She Wrote" or "Fresh Vegetable" one. *Yeah.* The "Fresh Vegetable" riddim—that could get me doing the Bogle in bed. Thinking about the riddim alone puts a song in my head.

Love yuh like fresh vegetable
So tell me if you love Tony Rebel

Meh love yuh like fresh vegetable
So tell me if you love Tony Rebel[24]

I'm automatically flooded with memories that manifest as dance moves that were in vogue during the early 1990s, when

[22] Stupid.

[23] Riddim refers to an instrumental track that is used to accompany different songs. Riddims assist DJs in moving effortlessly from one song to a next.

[24] Tony Rebel, "Fresh Vegetable."

this riddim emerged. I tick. I Bogle. I wine (always); I can't help it. And then my brain, like a DJ, starts to mix in the next song.

Hey little girl,
Each time you pass my way,
I'm tempted to touch

The dress you wear,
Your perfume,
Keeps me wanting you so much[25]

Beres stays on my mind for a little bit, but then I can't help but mix in some Richie Stephens.

Ooo the shape I'm in
And would you believe I've lost the race again
But I'm coming again 'cause I just gotta get in
Cause I'm tryin' to get to you[26]

On one riddim, you could have any number of songs, and they never seemed to get old. It's a modern take on an old African tradition of creating something new from the old and adding slight variations to music to keep it interesting. Creativity surely survived our journey across the seas.

Cue: "My Adidas," Run DMC

The music played in East Flatbush and other West Indian neighborhoods was (and still is) distinct from other ethnic enclaves in New York City, but in many ways our neighborhood was like a lot of black American and Latino neighborhoods in the city. Like a Venn diagram, there were spaces

---

[25] Beres Hammond, "Tempted to Touch."

[26] Richie Stephens, "Trying to Get to You."

where musical tastes, styles, and attitudes intersected, particularly for the youth.

In the 1980s, brothers walked around like "Radio Raheem," blasting the latest in hip-hop, R&B, and freestyle from their boomboxes. Ladies sported gold "door knocker" earrings and both men and women adorned their necks with rope chains. Cats wore Adidas and Pumas on their feet and fuzzy Kangol hats on their heads. When acid wash was in style, we sported it on our jeans, jackets, and shirts. And as the 1980s gave way to the 1990s, our fashion gave way too. Out came the baggy oversized clothes and the bright hues of Cross Colours. Later Karl Kani and Walker Wear came into fashion. We were part of a city that had a style, and we embraced it.

But these were perhaps the styles of the younger folk. Now, there are some people who feel they are forever young and will try to keep up with kids half their age, but my parents surely didn't wear baggy pants and Cross Colours. And they didn't listen to hip hop. But their "old people" music played side-by-side next to ours, creating a space with musical layers—West Indian, American, young, old—it was all there for our sonic consumption.

A History Lesson: How We Got Here

East Flatbush wasn't always a Caribbean enclave. Like so many of the Brooklyn neighborhoods that are now home to West Indian migrants—Flatbush, Canarsie, Crown Heights—East Flatbush was once primarily Jewish. Growing up, you could still see a few of the last remnants of Jewish life in the forms of elderly men and women who, for whatever reason, never left with the mass exodus; pardon the pun. Some old synagogues, like the one at the corner of Remsen Avenue and Avenue A, still exist, though they no longer function as

Jewish houses of worship.[27] I don't know why, but I used to like seeing those old Jewish men and women strolling down the street with their canes and walkers. There's still a sizeable Jewish community in Crown Heights, but they've been all but gone from East Flatbush and the other areas for quite some time. Now, if I see a white person in my neighborhood, I'm suspicious. I'm afraid of gentrification. But I'm getting ahead of myself.

West Indians have been coming to the United States, and New York City in particular, long before the development of West Indian enclaves like East Flatbush. However, the turn of the twentieth century marked the beginning of what would be deemed the "first wave" of West Indian migration to the United States. Prior to 1899, immigration statistics were limited in scope. It wasn't until immigration authorities began keeping records that provided "fairly detailed information about not only the provenance, but also the 'race' and ethnicity—as well as other characteristics, such as literacy, age, sex, and occupation—of those who migrated to the United States" that it became possible "to trace, with reasonable accuracy, the migration of people from the Caribbean to America."[28]

Although these new statistics were an improvement from previous ones, they were not flawless. Even today, record-keeping systems that are used in the United States, particularly census reports and statistics by the Immigration and Naturalization Service (INS), employ categories that are incomplete and/or "clash" with immigrant identities.[29] For example, INS statistics list immigrants separately according to "country of birth" and "state of residence." Race and ethnicity are not included in those statistics, making it more difficult (though not impossible) to accurately conduct any comprehensive study of

[27] The former synagogue now houses a church—Grace Deliverance Tabernacle, C.O.G.

[28] Winston James, *Holding Aloft the Banner of Ethiopia: Caribbean Radicalism in Early Twentieth-Century America* (London and New York: Verso, 1999), 8.

[29] Waters, *Black Identities*, 49.

West Indian immigrants that includes those two identifiers. In addition, INS statistics do not include undocumented immigrants.

In contrast, U.S. census reports are more comprehensive and include separate categories for race, ancestry, and birthplace. However, West Indians are subsumed in categories labeled "foreign-born blacks," which do not distinguish between blacks from the Caribbean, Africa, or elsewhere. Non-black West Indians, including whites, ethnic Chinese, Indians, Syrians, and Lebanese, are subsumed in similar racial categories for the "foreign-born." In addition, categories that list immigrants by country of origin underestimate the size of the West Indian community "by missing English-speaking West Indians from enclave communities in predominantly Hispanic nations and those holding British passports," as well as people like me, born in the United States to West Indian parents.[30] Nonetheless, scholars do the best they can with the information available to them.

Prior to 1924, immigration to the United States from the Western Hemisphere was unlimited,[31] and West Indian migration to the United States increased steadily until that year, when the number of West Indians arriving in the country peaked at 12,243.[32] Then, the passing of the 1924 Immigration Act placed several restrictions on immigration, subsequently reducing the numbers of West Indians entering the country. The new law restricted the number of people entering the U.S. based on national origin.

---

30 Philip Kasinitz, *Caribbean New York: Black Immigrants and the Politics of Race* (Ithaca and London: Cornell University Press, 1999), 15. It should be noted that the census does take into account members of the "native" population who are of "foreign or mixed parentage." However, again, West Indians are lumped into categories that privilege race over nationality/regional heritage. See Dianne Schmidley, "Profile of the Foreign Born Population in the U. S.: 2000," *United States Census Bureau,* U.S. Department of Commerce, 24, accessed August 16, 2015, http://www.census.gov/content/dam/Census/library/publications/2001/demo/p23-206.pdf.

31 Waters, *Black Identities*, 34.

32 Kasinitz, *Caribbean New York*, 24.

> The quota provided immigration visas to two percent of the total number of people of each nationality in the United States as of the 1890 national census. It completely excluded immigrants from Asia.[33]

Despite these restrictions, a sizeable number of West Indians continued to migrate "through the underutilized British quota."[34] This trend continued until the Great Depression, when large numbers of West Indian immigrants left the United States. Between 1932-1937, more West Indians left the United States than had entered during that time period.[35]

Besides the 1924 immigration restrictions and the Great Depression, other factors contributed to a decline in West Indian migration to the United States that lasted until 1965. In 1952, the United States issued the McCarran-Walter Act, which "restricted the use for the 'home country' quotas by colonial subjects."[36] Thus, West Indians who wished to enter the United States under the British quota were severely hampered. In effect, the McCarran-Walter Act made it virtually impossible for West Indians to enter the United States unless they were related to persons who had previously migrated.[37]

The upsurge in migration after 1965 was primarily the result of two factors: the tightening of British immigration laws coupled with the easing of immigration laws in the United States. In 1962, following the independence of its two largest colonies in the Caribbean—Jamaica and Trinidad—Britain placed "severe" restrictions on immigration from the Com-

---

[33] Office of the Historian, "Milestones: 1921-1936," *Office of the Historian*, U.S. State Department, accessed August 16, 2015, https://history.state.gov/milestones/1921-1936/immigration-act. I won't get into the racism of some of these policies.

[34] Kasinitz, *Caribbean New York*, 24.

[35] Ibid.

[36] Ibid., 26.

[37] Ibid.

monwealth.[38] According to Karl Miller, the Commonwealth Immigrants Act was passed "to limit the admission of those who wished to leave the West Indies and come to Britain with their black and brown faces to fill the jobs that needed to be filled."[39] Prior to that year, West Indian migration to Britain had been unrestricted, and many West Indians migrated to England during the years that United States immigration laws were most stringent.[40] However, in 1965, three years after the Commonwealth Immigrants Act was passed, the United States introduced the Hart-Cellar Immigration Reform Act, which ended the national origins quota system and in effect paved the way for large numbers of West Indians to enter the country.[41] As England closed its doors to West Indians, the United States opened theirs, and thousands of West Indians took advantage of the opportunity.

My family was part of that post-1965 wave, where West Indians began arriving in New York en masse and settling in Central Brooklyn. These immigrants created a little bit of "home" in a part of the world that seemed so removed from the lifestyle from which they came. This is the world I was dropped into one day in 1979. East Flatbush became my neighborhood, my community. And although there were certain things that I would learn on the streets of East Flatbush, some things I could only learn at home from my family.

[38] Ibid.

[39] Karl Miller, introduction to *A House for Mr. Biswas*, by V.S. Naipaul (New York: Knopf, 1995), vii.

[40] Kasinitz, *Caribbean New York*, 26.

[41] Ibid., 27.

Chapter 2:
There's No Place Like Home

Back in the days when I was young
I'm not a kid anymore
But some days I sit and wish
I was a kid again.
—Ahmad, "Back in the Day"

Back in the Day

Cue: "Back in the Day," Ahmad

There are times when I long to be a kid again. It's only when you grow up that you understand why the old heads used to tell you, "Don't try and grow up too fast," or "Enjoy your youth." Time surely flies, or as my grandmother once told me, "No child. It is we who fly by."

> *Back in the days when I was young*
> *I'm not a kid anymore*
> *But some days I sit and wish*
> *I was a kid again*

Those lines play back in my mind like a cassette in a Walkman—the only lyrics I can recall, and the only ones that mattered—and I'm transported to that apartment on East 54th

Street, my first home. Well, at least the first home that I can remember.

Technically, my first home was the apartment on Farragut Road that my mom would point out to me on occasion when we'd walk or drive by that stretch of Brooklyn. I was only a few months old when the apartment was burglarized, and my parents promptly decided to leave. That's when we moved to East 54th Street.

We moved into a spacious one-bedroom apartment on the top floor of a three-story building. There were four of us—me, Mom, Dad, and my older brother, David—but the apartment didn't seem cramped. The bedroom was large—big enough to fit a queen-sized bed for my parents and a set of bunk beds for David and me. Sometimes my parents would sleep on the guest bed, a pull-out bed that they had placed in the foyer of the apartment, which doubled as an office. Before I started school, I spent many hours looking out of the window in the far left corner of the bedroom. The window faced the street, and as I looked out, I would sometimes see my brother's kindergarten class having recess in the playground of the school on Clarkson Avenue. Emma Lazarus, P.S. 268. That would soon be my elementary school, too. It's almost fitting that the first school I'd ever attend was named after the woman whose famous poem graces the Statue of Liberty, the symbol of immigrant hope and pride.

There were two other windows in the bedroom that faced the street. They opened out onto a fire escape that David and I once tried to use to run away. David "did get *boof*"[1] by my parents, and he decided that he no longer wanted to live at home; I figured I would join him for the ride. Clearly we had been watching too many cartoons. We gathered up whatever belongings we wanted to take and secured them in a bindle. With our makeshift bags complete, we threw them over our shoulders. We were ready. We planned to climb out through the fire escape, and we would have too, except for the lock on

[1] To "boof "or "boof up" means to insult, belittle, or shame a person.

the gate encasing the window.

Stuck inside, we spent much of our playtime in that bedroom. The living room was reserved mostly for watching television, playing music, and entertaining guests. Our living room was huge, even by today's standards, with a few windows overlooking a courtyard facing Clarkson Avenue. It was perfect for the elaborate birthday celebrations that my parents used to throw us before my dad became very religious, and those fêtes were replaced with cottage (prayer) meetings.

The apartment was nice, but we were by no means rich. The fact that my brother and I collected roaches for pets, and I frequently hunted mice with my dad, is probably an indicator of the latter. To save money, my parents collected packets of salt, pepper, ketchup, and other condiments that we got whenever they treated us to McDonald's or Popeye's, which was rarely. And Sunday dinner was always at Grandma's because my parents couldn't afford a traditional Trinidad Sunday meal that included stew chicken, macaroni pie, and callaloo.[2]

Some people might have considered us poor, but I don't think that ever occurred to me. We were financially strapped, perhaps, but I was well-clothed, well-fed, and well-bred. My mother often says, "When you ent have mammy, suck granny," meaning that one needs to make do with what one has. And my parents did. With each passing year, I have more respect for the way that they raised us—their children—making sacrifices that others would not have made, and instilling in us important values.

The Kung Fu Fighter and the Minister

Cue: "Kung Fu Fighting," Carl Douglas

I remember the day I was born. No one seems to believe me when I say this, but I don't really care too much. I know it to be true, and nothing anyone else tells me can make me unknow it.

[2] A local dish described further in Chapter 3.

On the day I was born, I remember seeing my dad. He was smiling wildly at me with that wide smile he makes when he is very happy or laughing at one of his own very corny jokes. Dad is a pastor of a Pentecostal church. Well, now he is. When I was born, he was relatively new to the church, having grown up, for the most part, as a non-practicing Catholic. Not sure what he would have thought then, but now Dad doesn't believe in reincarnation. However, my father was Chinese in a past life. Of this, I am certain.

Aspects of his past life seeped into our present world, and David and I were fed a heavy diet of Kung Fu movies, so much so that (to the shock of some East Asian Studies majors at my college) I could determine with much success the time period in which Chinese movies were set based on the clothing of the actors.

"Wow. Where did you learn that?"

"Kung Fu movies."

Of course David and I watched the blockbuster films that made Bruce Lee a star—"Enter the Dragon," "The Big Boss," and "Game of Death," among others. But we also watched films that included Kung Fu stars that were lesser known in the United States—Alexander Fu Sheng, Gordon Liu, and young martial artists who would later gain Hollywood fame, such as Jackie Chan, Donnie Yen, Jet Li, and Michelle Yeoh.[3] As a child, and even later as an adult, I would boast that I had viewed hundreds of Kung Fu movies.

However, my dad was not merely interested in watching Kung Fu on the silver screen or television; he trained as well. We accompanied him to staged Kung Fu demonstrations, complete with light effects, where he and his Kung Fu brothers would present a show of their fighting skills. My father at-

---

[3] In some of her earlier films, she was billed as "Michelle Khan." Also, properly speaking, Michelle Yeoh is not a trained martial artist. However, her background as a dancer prepared her to do most of her own stunts. "Biography: Michelle Yeoh," *IMDb*, accessed August 16, 2015, http://www.imdb.com/name/nm0000706/bio?ref_=nm_ov_bio_sm.

tempted to pass those skills on to us, his progeny. On Saturday mornings, David and I would get up early, and before we were even allowed to eat breakfast, we were required to practice. We learned several stances, punches, and kicks, and were so strong that while still in single digits, we could perform push-ups on our fingertips. As a result, I thought I was a real *bad-john*.[4] At no more than five years old, I would stick my head out our apartment window and yell at the young men who had a penchant for sitting on my dad's car. (For some reason, sitting on other people's cars was common throughout the 1980s and early 1990s.) I would threaten these car sitters with verbal threats and a plastic bat. On several occasions, I'd even have a plastic bat ready for my dad when he came home from work. Although my dad never encouraged my vigilante behavior, on at least two occasions he did beat up some men who attempted to rob us. As I got older, perhaps due to the growing influence of the church in our lives, the badjohn in me got quieted. However, the discipline I learned through the practice of martial arts would serve me well later in life.[5]

Unlike Mom, Dad doesn't have much of an accent, but there are words that he says that hint to an astute listener that he is not from this country. One day when I was in my late teens, my younger sister—who must have been about three or four at the time—was busy walking back and forth between my grandmother's room, where I had been fixing my hair, and my parents' bedroom, where my dad had been watching an action movie. We had long since moved from the apartment on East 54th Street and were now living in a house in a different section of East Flatbush. During one of my sister's trips back to my parents' bedroom, my dad was watching a scene in which a

---

[4] A person who exhibits violent or rough behavior.

[5] My father had a love affair with all things Chinese, not just Kung Fu. He made attempts at learning the language, and Chinese food was always his first choice when we'd go out to eat. But perhaps most telling is the fact that my father, a homebody, would gladly leave house and home for one of two adventures—a trip to outer space and, you guessed it, a trip to China.

series of bombs were going off.

"Dad. What's that?" my sister asked.

"A grennid," he replied.

"A grennid?" I thought to myself, "What the heck is that?" I stood confused for a few seconds before finally yelling, "A grenade, Dad! A grenade!"

"That's what I said!"

That always seemed to be his response. I shook my head and thought, "Lawd, he's gonna make this child grow up saying all kind a wrong thing." Some of the words my father would say made us joke that he *had* to be "from country." (He wasn't.)

My father arrived in the United States in 1974 after his mother, Grandma Helen, had sent for him and his younger brother. She had married an American and so was able to obtain a green card and later visas for her children. That same year, while attending Brooklyn College, my father met my mother, who had arrived in New York one year prior and was living in Brooklyn with her mother, brother, and toddler sister.

My Mother's Accent

As a child, sometimes I would watch my mom as I sat and played, and I'd wonder what it was like to be her, not just to walk around in her body, but to *be* her. What did she think? What did she feel? It would be well over a decade before I understood the significance of these moments, which foreshadowed my developing a heightened empathic sense later in life. But I digress.

My mother was a snob, or at least so I thought. "I went to Bishop Anstey High School," she would frequently assert with pride. Bishop's—as it is often called—was an elite, all-girls, Anglican school where British expatriates would send their children to be educated. When my mother began attending in 1965, the school had only recently become integrated, and young Trinidadians like my mother had a lot to prove. Despite making "the marks," these young women were determined to demonstrate that they were in no way inferior to their British peers.

It would take several years, but I eventually would learn that my mother is not a snob but a woman who came of age during a period in Trinidad and Tobago when the entire nation had something to prove. With independence being successfully attained on August 31, 1962, Trinbagonians felt the need to demonstrate to Great Britain (and the world) that they—people cloaked in black and brown bodies—were not only intelligent and talented, but also fit for self-governance. But I'll talk a bit more about this later.

Mom was the erudite of the family. She was slim, but naturally so, and far from athletic. She couldn't have cared less about activities of a physical nature—she left that to Dad—and was mostly concerned with her children receiving a proper education. I sometimes joke that had my father raised us according to his desires, my brother, sister, and I would have been meatheads. Had my mother solely been tasked with the responsibility, my siblings and I would have been all brains and no brawn.

My mother has what can be deemed a thick accent, and it says a lot about who she is as a person. She speaks with a "Trini" accent in casual settings—at home or with her friends. However, she often switches to a decidedly British accent (and speaks "the Queen's English") when she answers the phone or speaks formally. Despite being fully aware that my mother has an accent, it wasn't until I was in the seventh or eighth grade that the fact truly resonated with me. My mother had an *accent*—not just one that my brother and I mimicked mercilessly, but one that others heard as well.

One evening, a classmate called my house. My mother had answered the phone, and once I had retrieved it, the voice on the other end said, "Wow! Your mother has a strong accent! Is she Jamaican?"

"No, she doesn't!" I said defensively. "And she's not Jamaican. She's from Trinidad!"[6]

Why did the fact that someone expressed that my mother has an accent trouble me? I can't say for certain. But my mother's speech—her accent, syntax, and vocabulary—functioned as a pathway connecting my siblings and me to her birthplace, keeping us rooted to our families still living in her homeland, as well as to those who have long since passed on. The words she spoke, we *nyamed*[7] them down until they became a part of us.

My mother always told me that when she came to this country, she was determined not to lose her accent. You see, her accent was part of her culture, and she was determined to maintain both. She was also determined that my siblings and I would know our culture, and that the best way to do this was through education.

Emma Lazarus

Here's to the school we love
The finest in the land
Where all the children are
A bright and happy band
Let all the things we do
And records we may make
Add to the glory of
Our own Two Sixty-Eight!
—School Anthem, Emma Lazarus, P.S. 268

[6] When unsure, always ask where the person is from rather than making an assumption. People who are not from Jamaica get tired of being asked if they are Jamaican, or worse, asked if the country of their birth (or heritage) is in Jamaica.

[7] To "nyam" something down means to eat it quickly or "gobble" it up.

Elementary school was fun. Nonetheless, I made many attempts to go home, especially in kindergarten. In those days, I used to feign illness so I could go home to be with my dad. The last time I recall pulling such a stunt was in second grade. I told my teacher I didn't feel good. (I felt fine.) As I stood before her in front of the class, she placed the back of her hand over my forehead and said, "You feel warm." She immediately sent me to the nurse, who said I had a fever. For some reason, all of the times that I pretended to be sick, the medical staff concluded that I indeed was sick. The relationship between mind and body would become a growing fascination in years to come, but I digress.

Emma Lazarus, P.S. 268—that was my school. It may not have been the best in the nation, but it was good enough. There were no lotteries or people fighting to get in. We were all just expected to be there because it was our "zone" school, our neighborhood school. Most of the kids in the school were black, either of West Indian or black American heritage. Those who were black American generally had parents and/or grandparents from the southern parts of the United States. I don't remember any white or non-black Hispanic kids in attendance.[8] If they were there, they were a significant minority.

The administrators, teachers, and staff were a more diverse bunch. Many of them were Jewish, a reminder that the demographics of the neighborhood in which we lived were once quite different. It also reflected the fact that Jews had been and continue to be a dominant force in New York City public schools, even despite the fact that their representation in the student body has dwindled considerably. We had black teachers—West Indians and black Americans—though I never had a West Indian teacher while in attendance there.

To this day, I have a lot of respect for the teachers at that school. These weren't teachers with a savior complex. They left me with no impression that they were trying to save the disadvantaged "inner city" children. Yes, they were there for a pay-

[8] There were likely Panamanians of West Indian descent who attended.

check, but they also simply did their jobs to the best of their abilities. They taught us what we needed to know, enough that many of us later tested into Philippa Schuyler, a school for the gifted and talented that at the time was consistently one of the top three middle schools in the city.

A lot of our socialization took place during school hours, particularly during recess when we'd go outside and let loose. Adults never immersed themselves in our play. I'm sure they were around monitoring the playground, but they were all but invisible to me. We played many types of games, but several rounds of tag were usually ripe for the occasion. To find out who was "It," we would all stick our right feet out and form a circle of feet, toes touching. Then we would recite one of several chants while one person tapped each toe in succession, on the beat.

Engine Engine Number 9
Going down Chicago Line
If my train falls of the track,
Do you want your money back?

Stop. Everyone looks at the person whose foot was last tapped. Will they say yes or no?

"Yes."

"Y-E-S-SPELLS-YES-AND-OUT-YOU-MAY-GO-FOR-THE-REST-OF-NINE-TEEN-EIGHT-Y-SIX."

Whoever's toe was touched last could step out—that person was not "It." Then we'd begin chanting again, as one of us tapped the remaining feet until only one foot was left. We might repeat the original chant, or use a new one.

Mickey Mouse built a house.
How many bricks did he put in?

Stop. Everyone looks at the person whose foot was last tapped. How many bricks will they say?

"Eight."

"1-2-3-4-5-6-7-8."

The person whose toe was tapped on "8" might be out, or you could add a sort of coda, like:

Not because you're dirty
Not because you're clean
Just because you kissed the boy (girl)
Behind the dirty magazine

After repeating the process several times, the person with the last remaining foot was the dreaded "It."

Both boys and girls played tag, but we also had games that were more gender-specific. The girls spent time jumping rope—singles and double dutch. I usually found myself playing singles since I was one of the unfortunate *double-handed*[9] members of the group. Ironically, I could turn and jump scotch,[10] but that was rarely played.

If we weren't jumping rope, we (the girls) were likely playing some sort of hand-clapping game, like "Down, down, baby, down goes the roller coaster." We clapped hands together while chanting about Miss Mary Mack and Rockin' Robin, and about not wanting to go to Mexico no more.

We also learned school cheers.

S-U-C-C-E-S-S!
That's the way we spell success
Put it together and you will see
The Lazarus Angels can't be beat
Sound off 1-2! Sound off 3-4!
Now hit it!

We chanted, sang, danced, and clapped throughout recess.

---

[9] Double-handed was the term that was used to refer to those who could not properly turn the rope.

[10] Scotch was similar to double-dutch except the rope was turned out instead of in.

This is how we learned rudimentary music skills like clapping on beat, moving on the beat, *staying* on beat, and adjusting to complex rhythmic patterns. Most importantly, this was how we built friendships and learned how to interact with others in groups. People love to talk about the musicality of black people as though we are just born clapping and singing. Not so. Music is an integral part of the upbringing of most people of African descent. In a culture where children are exposed to music at a young age, a certain musicality develops. However, believe you me, there are plenty of black people with "no rhythm," and perhaps even more who can't hold a tune. Nonetheless, being a part of a culture where group participation is not just welcomed, but encouraged means that most children will feel comfortable participating in musical activities.

Off the playground, we learned the basics—how to read, write, and do arithmetic. Our teachers taught us about important historical figures, which included a large number of African Americans who contributed to life in the United States. There were the requisites like Harriet Tubman, Martin Luther King, Jr., and Malcolm X. We also learned about Mary McLeod Bethune, Madame C.J. Walker, Benjamin Banneker, George Washington Carver, and Booker T. Washington. My early formal education taught me that black people were more than former slaves. We were teachers, scientists, entrepreneurs, artists, and athletes. Our legacy in the United States was not merely one of a downtrodden people, but rather of a people who had *overcome* almost two hundred fifty years of slavery and another one hundred years of Jim Crow.[11] Though my early education exposed me to African American history,

[11] The year 1619 marks when Africans were first recorded to have been sold into slavery in the British colonies in North America. This sale in African bodies took place in Jamestown, Virginia. Slavery continued on what would later become U.S. soil until 1865, when the 13th Amendment to the Constitution—which prohibited slavery—was ratified. The Civil Rights Act of 1964 and the Voting Rights Act of 1965 were passed in an effort to end to Jim Crow. However, race-based discrimination has persisted in the form of more subtle acts such as housing and job discrimination, and an escalation in the criminalization of black and brown bodies.

my formal schooling in Caribbean history and culture would not occur until I attended college. Before then, I attended "the school of Ma."

The School of Ma

I was enrolled in "the school of Ma" at birth, and it's doubtful that I will ever graduate. It's not that I'm a dull student. It's just that there is always more to learn. My schooling at Emma Lazarus was often supplemented with my mother's teachings. One of my earliest memories consisted of my mom's suggestion that I make civil rights activist and Trinidadian native Stokely Carmichael (later known as Kwame Ture) the subject of my Black History Month book report.

While some of Mom's lessons came in the form of direct conversations, many of them were made poignant through song.

"Yuh doh know dat one?" my mother would ask before erupting in verse.

Well the girls in town feeling bad
No more Yankees in Trinidad
They going to close down the base for good
Them girls have to make out how they could

Brother is now they park up in town
In for a penny, and in for a pound
Believe me it's competition for so[12]
Trouble in the town when the price drop low[13]

My mother introduced me to the U.S. presence in Trinidad during World War II by singing "Jean and Dinah," a well-

[12] "For so" is a phrase that denotes a lot of something. "Rain for (fuh) so" is an expression that means it is raining heavily.

[13] Mighty Sparrow, "Jean and Dinah."

known calypso by Slinger Francisco, more popularly known as the Mighty Sparrow. She would later explain that, as part of the Lend-Lease Act with Great Britain, the U.S. was permitted to lease land in Trinidad for a period of ninety-nine years, until the early termination of that agreement by Dr. Eric Williams.[14] In my mother's words, Dr. Williams told the Americans to "get the hell out." "Jean and Dinah" is not only about prostitution, but also some of the ways that colonialism and imperialism have contributed to the destabilization of Trinidad society. Mom used the song as a teaching tool.

More songs would follow, each one teaching me about a different aspect of Trinidad history and culture—the collapse of the West Indies Federation, racial conflict in Trinidad, obeah, and more. My mother has always had a habit of singing history, and she always seems to have a calypso for every occasion. There's no shortage of songs in her arsenal. And though my mother could not (and still cannot) sing to save her life, I have to give her credit. (As she would say, "Give Jack his jacket.") You see, my mother is the embodiment of oral tradition at its finest. She is a modern day griot with an impeccable memory and the desire and ability to maintain history through song. One has to understand that my mother was doing this in an age prior to compact discs, the Internet, and mp3s. She calls upon the most appropriate song for any occasion, and she imparts knowledge to all who are willing to hear.

People think that school is the primary place where one learns. The truth is, it's in the home. The education that I received from my mom was invaluable and by far trumps what I ever learned in school. I learned not only facts from Mom, but also values. However, not all of these lessons were acquired through the gentleness of a song. There were other ways, much harder ways, in which I learned.

---

[14] Dr. Eric Williams was the former Premier and first Prime Minister of Trinidad and Tobago.

The Cuttail

Cuttail
n. a rite of passage for almost all West Indian children.

"Your ass is grass."

That was a favorite line of my parents. The cleaner version was, "Your behind is mine." Ah…growing up in a West Indian household. At least my parents didn't make me kneel on rice grains. It seems like everyone from a West Indian family has fond memories of at least one cuttail.

Now, the cuttail is not an experience exclusive to children of West Indian heritage. African American and Latino children have similar experiences, as do those of other racial and ethnic backgrounds, even if they call the experience by a different name. Beat, whipped, spanked—whatever you want to call it—my friends and I had experienced it many times, and we all had stories that we wanted to share, stories of comparison, almost to see who had it worse. Though undoubtedly many children experience physical abuse at the hands of their guardians, for most of us the "licks" we received weren't tantamount to abuse. It was a matter of reaping what we had sown; it was also an affirmation of our culture. Many of our parents grew up with the Biblical notion of "spare the rod, spoil the child."

> Those who spare the rod of discipline hate their children. Those who love their children care enough to discipline them.[15]

So the Bible provided justification for the cutting of little tails all across the globe, and it was all done in the name of love. Before giving us licks, my father would often say, "You think I want to beat you? This is gonna hurt me more than

[15] Proverbs 13:24 (New Living Translation).

it hurts you." Somehow, I think our butts hurt more than his broken heart.

Nowadays, social media is abuzz with talks about and images of parents shaming their children. However, my mother was the original child shamer, and she didn't need a video camera to do it. I don't even remember what we did in many of those instances, but my mom, at the top of her lungs and with her very Trini accent would bawl, "Allyuh want me to embarrass yuh here today?" or, "I will embarrass yuh you know!" She was loud, very loud. People would turn and stare. Already embarrassed, we were reduced to silence, thinking it best to quit while we were still, marginally, ahead. As my father used to like to say, "Who doh hear will *feel*." And we did, whether on a psychological or physical level.

While I wouldn't call what my brother and I experienced abuse, I will say that some cuttails were clearly unnecessary. It seemed like my parents could find any reason to give us licks—a spilled drink, not eating all of our food. Even laughing or playing too loudly could become a potential crime. Nonetheless, there were times when a cuttail was well deserved. And most of the time, a cuttail was the inevitable result of disobedience.

Tryin' your best to bring the water to your eyes
Thinking it might stop her from whipping your behind
—"I Wish," Stevie Wonder

Cue: "I Wish," Stevie Wonder

"Don't take that out there," my mother said to me as an aside from her phone conversation.

"I won't spill it," I assured her with my six-year old logic.

"If you spill it, yuh gonna get a cuttail," my mom responded.

I sat down in the hallway, and took a sip of my drink. I then carefully placed the cup on the ground next to me. Somehow, my leg met the cup, and the rest was history. I high-tailed it out of there. My mom chased me. I ran into the bathroom where my brother was taking a shower. Then, for some not so bright reason, I opened the door to see if my mother had gone. She hadn't. She grabbed me from out of the bathroom and *cut my tail.*

Parents have their own styles or approaches to the cuttail. My mother was a reflex beater. She'd get you in the moment. You'd be whacked before you even had a chance to think about what you had done. My father's approach was a little bit different. He made sure you had time to think about your actions and the resulting consequences.

"Now, what should I do with you?" my father asked as he sat on the bed with both David and me standing between his legs, facing him just below eye level.

"You…should…give…us…a…beat-ing," was our usual response, barely getting the words out in between sobs.

"Go get the belt," Dad said.

And so it began. As the licks commenced, Dad no longer sat down. He stood up, towering over us like some mythic, god-like figure, almost as if to show his superior might.

"Didn't I…"

Whack!

"…tell you…"

Whack!

"…not to…"

Whack! Whack!

"…touch the…"

Whack!

"…television!"

Whack! Whack! Whack!

Yes. This was all over a television.

I'm not sure I remember how this saga started, but for some reason David and I were grounded. I was likely not older than six, as we had not yet moved from the apartment on East 54th Street. As part of our punishment, we were prohibited from watching television. Shortly after the implementation of our television ban, my dad stepped out of the apartment.

We were home alone. I'm not sure what went through David's mind, but I'm sure I thought something to the effect of, "What a fool. He can't stop us from watching TV, now." I'm sure a sinister grin emerged on my face, and an evil laugh erupted as I thought those thoughts. David and I promptly began to watch television. Who knows what we were watching. It didn't matter, because the meat of the story is in what happened next.

Dad was home. We heard him as he approached the apartment door. Quickly, we turned off the television and returned to our spots on the living room floor. My dad walked in. I imagine we said, "Hi, Dad," or something of the sort. He looked at us, and then calmly walked to the television. He placed one hand on top of the television set and said, "Who told you you could watch TV?"

So there you have it. Those are the events that led to the infamous cuttail mentioned above. That day, I garnered a new respect for my dad. He was *clearly* the smartest man in the world. Who would have thought that he would have felt the top of the television to see if it was warm? My young brain didn't know enough about televisions to have foreseen the inevitable outcome of our actions. No, Papa was no fool.[16]

I watched terrified as my brother squirmed on the floor as he received each lash of the belt. I cried, not so much because I felt his pain, but because I knew that his pain would soon be my pain. I can't really say I remember my dad ever beating us in anger, but my brother and I meting out our own punishment, procuring the belt that would soon sting our flesh, and then watching one get beat before the other was tantamount to psychological torture.

My brother and I have many more memorable cuttails stored in our collective memory. One place that seemed to be a cuttail-free zone was Grandma's house. There, we had a lot more room to run around and play with impunity, and play we did.

---

[16] During a subsequent television ban, I tried to "ice" the television in the minutes prior to my dad's return home. Luckily, he didn't check the television because my remedy didn't work too well.

Grandma's Place

"You's a badjohn or what?" my grandma said as I ran up the stairs.

I was very much a daredevil. No fear existed in me at the time. I did what I pleased, and in many ways I knew I was invincible.

We didn't live with my maternal grandmother and aunt until we moved from the apartment on East 54th Street. Before then, they lived no more than a ten-minute drive away in a different neighborhood in East Flatbush. My grandmother rented an upstairs apartment from a woman named Carol King. Aunty Carol, as we used to call her, was from St. Vincent but had lived in Trinidad for many years. She had two children, including Uncle Rudy, who lived upstairs in a room that was connected to Grandma's bedroom by a locked door. Aunty Carol lived on the first floor, but she also rented a basement apartment to "Bishop," a nice but mysterious fella who kept his hair neatly contained within one of those oversized dreadlock hats.

Aunty Carol's house was on Winthrop Street, the second to last of several row homes that faced the parking lot of the sanitation station. There was a tree planted in front of the house, just to the right of the front gate as one entered the property. It was encircled with stones, or maybe brick, I can't be too sure. But somehow I got it into my head that that tree was the Tree of Life or the Tree of Knowledge of Good and Evil. It was more likely to be the latter, since the owner of the house seemed to really know how to pull the wool over people's eyes. Aunty Carol wasn't a very nice person, and I don't just say that because she had a habit of addressing me with the greeting of, "Hello, mop-head." She was a woman who had a penchant for controlling people and situations. Despite her temperament (or maybe because of it), Aunty Carol lived to be well over 100 years old. In hindsight, I wouldn't be surprised if she was "wuking obeah."

I remember very little of the inside of her home, though it would later remind me of Dickens' description of Miss Havisham's house in *Great Expectations*. The place wasn't disheveled or filled with cobwebs, but there was a sort of desolate aura that pervaded the home. It was eerie, perhaps made all the more so by the dolls that sat on shelving in the dining room of her house; they always seemed to be looking at me, like I was in a creepy horror flick.

For some reason, my grandmother made Aunty Carol stay[17] for my aunt Bernadette, better known as "Bee." This probably explains why Bee was the one person who never seemed to be in Aunty Carol's crosshairs. Bee is the youngest of my grandmother's three children, and she was born in the U.S. She was only a few years older than David and me; so in many ways she was like our older sister.

When Bee was around, we were never cooped up inside the house. We didn't just get out of the house; we got off the block. We would walk to the corner store, where David and I liked to get comic books and bubble gum. We'd get ice cream at Mama's Fried Chicken at the corner of Winthrop and Nostrand—I'd get strawberry, David would get chocolate, and Bee would get pistachio. Sometimes, we'd walk further north along Nostrand Avenue to get currant rolls and hard dough bread at Allan's Bakery. We explored the world together, and it was fun. My aunt had a lot of freedom, and in general it seemed that my grandmother was a parent who extended a wide leash to her children. She didn't demand much of them. However, there was one stern warning that my grandmother would give consistently to her children.

"*Study your book,*" she'd say, knowing full well the value of a good education.

My grandmother worked in the hospital library in Trinidad. She first came to the U.S. in 1964 on a trip with teachers from Trinidad. She stayed in the country between two and three months with Eden Diaz and her family, who lived on

[17] "To stay" for a child means to serve as godparent.

Schenectady Avenue in East Flatbush. It would be three years before my grandmother returned with the intent of staying.

Like so many other West Indian women, when my grandmother arrived in New York City in 1967, she began working as a domestic for a white couple in Long Island. She was tasked with taking care of the house and minding the couple's two young children. In those days, green cards were easier to come by, and after receiving hers, my grandmother intended to continue working as a domestic for the aforementioned couple. They even agreed to pay for driving lessons for her. However, a conversation with a woman named Viola—who would later become one of her good friends—made her reconsider her options.

"You want to be working for a white couple for the rest of your life?"

Soon after, my grandmother "fired the wuk" and got a job working at Bell Atlantic, where she remained employed until her retirement in 1990.

My grandmother always struck me as a quiet, dignified woman. She dressed well and carried herself with pride. But she lived through the Great Depression, so her behavior often reflected the mindset of a woman who grew up without many of the comforts that we now take for granted.

Grandma was frugal, and she frequently recycled clothes—my clothes and everyone else's. Numerous times I would see her wearing an item of mine that was either long forgotten or (thought to be) discarded. Let no good thing go to waste. She would frequently scold my aunt for taking too much food and then not eating it all. To this day, I have a hard time throwing away food.

My grandmother had other habits that reflected her upbringing. For instance, she always kept a chamber pot, a reminder that she came from a time when one didn't always have easy access to a toilet. She would keep it under her bed, from which the faint smell of urine would sometimes emerge. The chamber pot was primarily reserved for urine and spit, but occasionally other items that needed to be discarded would be tossed in there and later dumped into the toilet bowl. As a kid, I couldn't understand why she just didn't go to the bathroom that was right outside her bedroom door. However, as I got older, I started to realize that old habits die hard, and when my mom told me about the conditions of the *yard* in which they lived, things started to make a lot more sense. But I'll get to that later.

Learning more about my grandmother's past also helped me to understand her fervent religious spirit, which would manifest in various ways. At night, her bedroom would have a mysterious glow from the flicker of a single candle that sat atop the tall chest of drawers in the room. It was one of those religious candles, on which was displayed a figure of the Archangel Michael drawing his sword to slay a demon. The light from the candle, mixed with the pungent smell of Florida Water that often permeated her room, seemed to heighten my senses and unnerve my sensitive spirit. Years later, when we moved in together, I'd see her putting white powder behind her bedroom door. As I got older, I learned that my grandmother had experienced many things growing up that led her to believe that evil exists in this world just as naturally as good, and she believed in protecting herself from such harm.

I can't say that my grandmother was very affectionate with us, but she was cool. We never got any licks from her, but every now and again she would assert her dominance. She would inveigle us to play games like "Pinchy-Pinchy-Pinchy" and "Mercy." In the former, players see who can pinch the hardest; Grandma always could. Mercy had a similar theme of causing pain. Two people squeeze each other's hands until one of them bawls "Mercy!" Grandma was a pro at that one, too. You could be on your knees screaming, "Mercy! Mercy!" and she wouldn't let go of your hand.

We had good times at my grandmother's place on Winthrop Street. Then, a few weeks after my seventh birthday, Grandma and Bee moved from that house, and we moved from our apartment on East 54th Street. We all moved into a semi-attached house in yet another section of East Flatbush.

A Trinidad Christmas in Brooklyn

"Look, Mom! Diwali! Diwali!" I shouted as I spied the magical lights that lit up the cold New York night. My mother had told me that Diwali was the Hindu festival of lights that took place in Trinidad, and somehow I imagined the Christmas lights that adorned the houses in our new neighborhood to be part of the Diwali celebrations. Our neighbors decorated the fronts of their homes with lights, wreaths, and nativity scenes. In those days, it snowed regularly during the winter, making the season all the more magical.

For as long as I can remember, Christmas in our home has been a spectacle. It became especially so when we left East 54th Street and moved into a house. I'm not sure if it was because my parents had more money or because we had more space for my mom to go "all out."

The ritual commences perhaps weeks—no, months—before Christmas. As soon as Christmas items become available in the stores, my mother is on the go, beginning the process of transforming our home into a winter wonderland. I would arrive home in the evenings to find that new wreaths had been bought, and newly purchased poinsettias were now lining the living room. It seemed as if every day there was a new object crowding the house. And in the days leading up to Christmas, our place looked a mess—and it remained that way until Christmas Day.

My parents did their best to provide us with a true Trinidad Christmas, preparing the house for the season and cooking foods just as they would have in Trinidad.

Cue: "Drink Ah Rum," Lord Kitchener; "Christmas Time," Salsoul Orchestra; "The Chipmunk Song," The Chipmunks; "Christmas Won't Be the Same this Year," The Jackson 5; "Silent Night," The Temptations

My brother and I would wake up early Christmas morning to the smell of ham and freshly baked bread. The house would be sparkling, the tree—perfect. During the night and wee hours of the morning, while David and I slept, my parents would stay up to complete the preparations. The house was cleaned from top to bottom, and new curtains were ironed and hung. My dad—the resident baker—finished making the black cake, periodically topping it with additional rum and sherry. Mom made sorrel and *ponche (de) crème*—essentially egg nog with *lots* of rum. One of the last things they would do before retiring for the night would be to put the salt ham—which had been soaking for days—on the stove to boil, before later placing it in the oven. They would have to get up periodically during the night to check on it, and at some point before David and I awoke, my dad would place in the oven the dough that he had previously kneaded, so we could have fresh bread for breakfast.

The morning consisted of David and me harassing our too-tired parents to wake up so we could open presents. Then we'd have breakfast with a hefty serving of "ham and eggs" and fresh bread. The remainder of the day consisted of Mom preparing Christmas dinner while we listened to an array of Christmas music. The top Christmas albums in the house were by The Jackson 5, Sal Soul, and The Chipmunks. But David and I were well versed in a wide array of Christmas hymns and carols, which we learned at church and in school—and, of course, from Mom.

Years later, I would become enamored with a style of Christmas music from Trinidad that my parents didn't play for us growing up, but that had somehow gotten into my blood. I began playing this music in the house at Christmastime, adding a new layer to our holiday soundtrack. More on this later.

The Soundtrack of My Youth

Cue: "Trinidad Paseo," Lovey's Trinidad String Band; "Sugar Bum Bum," Lord Kitchener

I can't say that I come from a family of musicians. However, I come from a musical family, and in some ways music flows through our blood. Grandma's father, Papa, was a violinist who used to play with the string bands that were popular during the first few decades of the 20th century. During my stays in Trinidad as an adult, I would set my *cuatro*[18] behind the bedroom door next to his violin to signify my solidarity with his musicality. Grandma Helen's first cousin is Ed Watson, the producer behind Lord Kitchener's hit "Sugar Bum Bum," and my cousin Sedi, an artist after my own heart, plays the steelpan.

Something of a musical nature must have trickled down to my siblings and me because as we walked to the bus stop on our way to school, David would sometimes start to freestyle, insulting me all the while. The rhymes were good. I just wished they weren't directed at me. My brother was, if you will, a "man-of-words,"[19] reflecting a long-held tradition in Africa and the diaspora of using and manipulating words into an art form. From blues and calypso, to bomba and hip hop, black people have a legacy of infusing music and text with coded messages, innuendos, puns, and *double entendres*. Sometimes these meanings are couched in humor. Other times, they're as serious as a call for enslaved Africans to revolt or a song about "stealing away" to freedom.[20] But we lived in modern times, and so we were steeped in the music of the day.

My brother David is two years older than me, and al-

---

[18] Small four-stringed guitar played in Trinidad and elsewhere in the Americas, esp. in Venezuela, Colombia, and Puerto Rico (where a ten-stringed derivative is most commonly played). In Trinidad, it has been used primarily to accompany calypso and parang music.

[19] "Man-of-words" is a term used by folklorist Roger D. Abrahams to refer to "an observable social type" whose "performances are typified by his willingness to entertain and instruct anywhere and anytime, to make his own occasions." The ability of the "man-of-words" "to use active and copious verbal performance to achieve recognition within his group is observable throughout Afro-American communities in the New World." Roger D. Abrahams, "Rapping and Capping: Black Talk as Art," in *Black America*, ed. John F. Szwed (New York and London: Basic Books, 1970), 134-135.

[20] "Steal Away" is the title of a well-known Negro spiritual. It is one of several whose coded language instructed slaves on when and/or how to escape to freedom.

though we were both musically inclined, our interest in the matter took slightly different paths. I am a musician—a vocalist first and foremost, though I play the piano and cuatro. I started learning the piano at age seven, and when I was eight years old I received a Yamaha keyboard for Christmas. I liked hearing and analyzing how music was put together.

My brother and I were a formidable group. We each wrote our own songs and starred in mock music videos. I had hits like "He's a Thief" and "Too Bad, So Sad." David's hits included "Ugly People," "Egg Head," and "Lady in Red (Peed Her Bed)." All of the songs had a distinctly eighties sound, and had we come of age in the new millennium, I'm sure we would have been young YouTube sensations.

David was a musician in his own right. He didn't take the path of learning the theoretical aspects of music, but he knew good music from the mediocre type; he had a good ear for that sort of thing. Unlike me—somewhat shy and reticent (even if people don't notice)—my brother has always been a performer. He could get up on a stage and blow everyone away, mixing and blending words into a smooth texture. David kept up with the entertainment side of music. He knew who sang what and the year that songs were released. (David was the one who corrected me when I insisted—based on the sounds of their voices—that Tracy Chapman was a man and that Lisa Stansfield was black.) He ordered popular magazines dedicated to hip hop and R&B; each new release of *Right On!* and *Word Up!*, and later *Source* and *Vibe*, made it into our home.

Cue: "The Message," Grandmaster Flash and the Furious Five; "Ladies First," Queen Latifah feat. Monie Love; "You Got What I Need," Biz Markie; "She Keeps on Passin' Me By," Pharcyde; "Around the Way Girl," L.L. Cool J; "I Got a Man," Positive K; "I Used to Love H.E.R.," Common Sense (a.k.a. Common); "Tennessee," Arrested Development

My brother and I listened to a lot of music—calypso, soca, reggae, dancehall, R&B, and freestyle. But I don't think it would be inaccurate to say that we were children of hip hop—when hip hop was *hip hop*. That is, when hip hop best represented the diversity of the black experience in New York. Yes, the music represented our struggles. And yes, the music reflected the violence that has now come to dominate perceptions of hip hop and, by extension, black people in the United States. But in those days, it was just as easy to hear songs about love and uplift, where black women and men, boys and girls, could see and hear their vulnerabilities in the hip hop songs and videos that were released. Hip hop was fun then, even geeky sometimes. It could be spiritual, rough around the edges, and romantic, too. It reflected all that we were back then, or at least it did not present us as one-dimensional. You didn't have to search too hard to find something that represented you.[21]

And it wasn't just the music. The artists themselves represented me: not only my city, but also my heritage. Unbeknownst to many, several hip hop artists who have emerged over the years have been West Indian or of West Indian descent—first generation Americans, like myself. And I'm not just talking about more recent artists like Nicki Minaj. Kool DJ Herc, Grandmaster Flash, Doug E. Fresh, KRS-One, Pepa from Salt-N-Pepa, Busta Rhymes, Biggie Smalls, and Foxy Brown are just a few of such artists. New generations of West Indian-descended people have been contributing to the artistic, social, and political legacies bequeathed to us by our predecessors—Marcus Garvey, Shirley Chisholm, Stokely Carmichael, Cicely Tyson, Geoffrey Holder, and Harry Belafonte, among others.

Cue: "You're All I Need," Marvin Gaye and Tammi Terrell; "Let's Stay Together," Al Green; "Precious Lord," Aretha Franklin; "Hold My Mule," Shirley Caesar; "God's Got It," Milton Brunson & the Thompson Community Singers; "Tomorrow," The Winans

Despite the fact that Mom was spitting out Sparrow lyrics every other day, I didn't grow up in a house where Caribbean music was played frequently. When I was a child, my parents

[21] Granted, I'm sure not everyone saw themselves represented in hip hop, but I would argue that the representation in those days was more varied than what's readily available today.

did not play calypso or the newly-emerging soca music. Instead, they listened to and played the popular black American music of the time, particularly R&B and soul. Marvin Gaye, Al Green, Aretha Franklin were household favorites. Later, as my father became more religious, a steady stream of gospel music flowed through the house or, more often, through the car radio. Shirley Caesar, Milton Brunson, the Winans, and countless other artists whispered in my ear and informed my musical journey.

Cue: "Tiney Winey," Byron Lee and the Dragonaires

A fair portion of the Caribbean music that I listened to came from outside of the home—from a car on the street or blasting from a nearby house party. We also heard the latest music from Trinidad and other islands by attending house parties. My brother's godmother, Aunty Janet, always seemed to have the best fêtes with the most current music, and my brother and I would eat it all up. As I got older, I would bring calypso and soca into our home via recorded music, purchased or received as a gift. Most of these cassettes, and later CDs, were bootleg copies of Caribbean music formatted into "mix tapes." They were widely available, and I know I had my share.

* * *

"This is D. Brown rocking the mic for you. Caller, can I take your request? Hello?"

"Hello?"

"Hello. Yes. Caller, you're on the air. Can I take your request?"

"Yes. Dis is Marcia. I want yuh tuh play 'Ah Home' by Iwer George, and I wanna send ah shout out to Mammy, Stacy, and Brian back home in Tunapuna. Big up TnT massive!"

"Ok. Thank you, Marcia, for calling in. Yes. Big up to all of Trinidad and Tobago and to the entire West Indian massive! Marcia, here is your request, and you know anywhere soca playin', 'Ah home!'"

* * *

A lot of the music that David and I listened to at home came from the radio, and Caribbean music was no different. Popular stations, like 98.7 Kiss FM, that mostly aired R&B and hip-hop dedicated some air time each week to playing Caribbean music. But perhaps the strongest radio presence for Caribbean music during my youth was WLIB 1190 AM, which specifically catered to the West Indian community.[22] It was through this radio station that one could hear the voices of the West Indian diaspora in New York City.

Through WLIB we listened to much more than just music. In the early 2000s, I started studying the station and noting various aspects of its programming. The station aired talk shows and commercials for products and events catering to the needs of West Indians living in the city. WLIB advertised health-conscious events, such as walks for prostate cancer, as well as programs for budding entrepreneurs, like those offered by the Small Business and Development Center at Baruch College. There were frequent promotions for popular Caribbean nightclubs, like the Elite Ark, and advertisements for Travelspan, a travel agency specializing in trips to and from the West Indies. Major corporations such as Burger King, JC Penney, and First Republic Mortgage Bank sought to broaden their clientele base by advertising to a West Indian audience via the station and using (with the exception of JC Penney) persons with unequivocally West Indian accents as the speakers in their commercials.

In many ways, WLIB was crucial in crystallizing the West Indian community in New York. DJs would implicitly define the community by the music they played and the islands they would "big up" (or shout out) on the air. Musical programming played a vital role in creating bonds (or breaking them) within the West Indian community. There were times when, as a young girl, I felt that WLIB did not play enough calypso and soca, and that my heritage was being marginalized in favor of reggae and dancehall, a sentiment that was echoed by others.

---

[22] WLIB no longer caters to the West Indian community.

My friend Tiffany, whose father is Trinidadian and mother Honduran, once told me she used to feel slighted by WLIB's programming:

> When WLIB used to play more…specifically Jamaican music, you know…I used to be like sitting there just waiting to hear some…music from my country and it would be…one in between four reggae songs.[23]

However, I should note that WLIB's programming became more inclusive over the years and consisted of music not only from Jamaica, Trinidad and Tobago, and Barbados, but also St. Vincent, Grenada, and Haiti as well. WLIB even began including a program—"Indo-Caribbean Today" with Amit Parasnath—dedicated to the East Indian community, which aired every Sunday morning from eight to ten. In many ways, the station grew to reflect the changing dynamics of the West Indian community in New York City.

While the music disseminated via WLIB helped to create bonds between different members of the West Indian community in New York, there were other aspects of the station's programming that helped to foster a sense of community. WLIB provided broadcasts to and from several West Indian countries, allowing listeners to hear live radio from their respective homelands and communicate with loved ones back "home." Listeners who called in to the radio program were able to send greetings and messages to family members living in their country of origin. Being able to communicate with loved ones was extremely important for many listeners, as talking to loved ones via the radio offset the cost of calling home directly, which in those days had the potential to be extremely expensive.

Equally important to listeners was the ability to receive up-to-date news information from their respective home countries, as well as general news information from the West Indies.

[23] Tiffany James, personal interview, 2003.

Tiffany said she liked WLIB in part because "as the day progresses, you actually get to hear international news, or news with a specifically West Indian perspective, which makes me feel a little closer to home. You know what I mean? It gives me a feeling of nostalgia."[24]

Together, the musical and non-musical aspects of WLIB, as well as those of several pirated stations that emerged over the years catering to the West Indian community, served to create a space where West Indians in New York could feel connected to their native lands from the privacy of their own homes. The music and information flowing from these stations contributed to altering the soundscape of New York City, bringing immigrants and first-generation Americans closer to "home." These radio stations created an environment that allowed many West Indian immigrants to simultaneously inhabit multiple spaces. For example, West Indians who live "ah foreign" could metaphorically occupy the space of their homelands through music, despite the reality that many would never be able to return home again.

Fortunately for me, my parents had their "papers," which meant they could leave the country freely without fear of being barred from re-entering. My father would only return to Trinidad once during my childhood, and I was almost thirty years old before we touched Trinidad soil at the same time. However, my mom made several trips to Trinidad during my youth, taking my brother and me on several of them. It was important that we learned about the land of her birth.

[24] Ibid.

Chapter 3:
Island in the Sun

This is my island in the sun
Where my people have toiled since time begun
I may sail on many a sea
Her shores will always be home to me

Oh island in the sun
Willed to me by my father's hands
All my days, I will sing in praise
Of your forest, waters, your shining sand
—"Island in the Sun," Harry Belafonte

Aunty Elaine died.

She died unexpectedly, and that's when my mom decided that she needed to take us to Trinidad. Aunty Elaine was the matriarch of the family. She was my maternal grandmother's eldest sister, and though I never met her, she's been with me all of my life. She has lived in our home and our hearts through the stories my mom has told about her. As I got older, I realized that many of my mom's mannerisms and habits—like her Christmas-time frenzy, her love of shopping, and her bossiness—were likely a direct result of the influence of Aunty Elaine in her life; they were all traits Aunty Elaine seemed to have had.

I made my first trip to Trinidad the summer after Aunty Elaine had died. Her death gave some urgency to my mother's need to have her children learn about the place of her birth. I think my mother was in many ways disappointed that I didn't have the opportunity to meet Aunty Elaine. She always said that Aunty Elaine would have liked me because I was "sassy." Yet the more I learned about Aunty Elaine over the years, the more I was certain we would have locked horns, but in a good way, like two sassy friends giving each other sass.

David had already traveled to the island as a baby. In 1978, during her final semester in college, my mother took the opportunity to finish her last credit in Trinidad at the University of the West Indies (UWI), St. Augustine. My brother was an infant, almost a year old, and so she brought him with her. Whatever recollection he had of his first trip to the island was miniscule, at best, but in 1984, my brother and I would embark on a journey of discovery—of self, family, and culture.

Portrait of Trinidad[1]

Cue: "Portrait of Trinidad," Mighty Sniper

I was born approximately 2,200 miles north of Port of Spain, the capital of Trinidad and Tobago, the land of my parents' birth. My heritage is a mix of Amerindian, African, and European, and my family's story goes beyond the borders of this twin-island nation. Our ancestors have navel strings buried throughout the Americas—in Dominica, Barbados, St. Vincent, and Venezuela. Nonetheless, I can only tell the history of the place with which I am most familiar, and so, Trinidad it is.

Trinidad is one half of the twin-island Republic of Trinidad and Tobago. The larger of the two islands, it is located just off the coast of Venezuela and is the southernmost island in the Caribbean. Trinidad is ethnically diverse, and while I was growing up, Mom would say that it is "the most cosmopolitan

---

[1] "Portrait of Trinidad" is the title of a song by the Mighty Sniper; my mother would often sing excerpts of the song to me.

island in the Caribbean." African, Indian, Chinese, Lebanese, Syrian, and "Spanish" all call Trinidad home.[2] We are commonly called a "callaloo nation," a reference to a food of the same name that incorporates several blended ingredients and that has become a metaphor for our diversity.[3]

The Land of Iere

San José, la primera capital de la isla Trinidad,
Por los índos fue llamado Caroni
Pero de Vera a los índios subyugó
Y San José la llamó en vez de Caroni
—"Historia de Trinidad," San Jose Serenaders[4]

Cue: "Historia de Trinidad," San Jose Serenaders

Prior to the arrival of Europeans, Trinidad was inhabited

[2] According to the most recent census report (2011), approximately 35.4 percent of the population identifies as East Indian, 34.2 percent identifies as African, and 22.8 percent identifies as mixed. The remaining ethnic groups, including Chinese, Syrians, Lebanese, and whites make up 1.4 percent of the population. In contrast, the ethnic make-up of Tobago is overwhelmingly African, with 85.2 percent of the population identifying as such. 8.5 percent of Tobago's population identifies as mixed. For more information, see Government of Trinidad and Tobago, Ministry of Planning and Sustainable Development, Central Statistical Office, *Trinidad and Tobago 2011 Population and Housing Census Demographic Report*, (Port of Spain, 2012), 15, cso.gov.tt.

[3] In Trinidad, callaloo is made with the callaloo (or dasheen) bush, "ochroes," pumpkin, and other foods, which are blended into a stew. Add pigtail or crab if so desired. "Tossed salad" has also been used as a metaphor for the nation, a reference to different cultural groups living side by side, as opposed to merging biologically and culturally. See Aisha Khan, *Callaloo Nation: Metaphors of Race and Religious Identity among South Asians in Trinidad* (Durham: Duke University Press, 2004) and Viranjini Munasinghe, *Callaloo or Tossed Salad: East Indians and the Cultural Politics of Identity in Trinidad* (Ithaca: Cornell University Press, 2001).

[4] The lyrics can be translated as: "St. Joseph, the first capital of Trinidad / The Amerindians called it Caroni / But de Vera subjugated the Amerindians / And called the place St. Joseph instead of Caroni."

by the indigenous people of the region, who are often divided into two large subgroups—the Arawak and Carib. To the Amerindians (as they are called locally), Trinidad was known as "Iere." For years the word was thought to have meant "Land of the Hummingbird." However, recent research has suggested that "Iere" is a misinterpretation of the indigenous word "kairi," which simply means island.[5]

The name "Trinidad" was given to the island in 1498 by Christopher Columbus, and popular lore suggests that as his ships approached the island, Columbus spotted in the distance three hills, which he viewed as representing the Holy Trinity—the Father, Son, and Holy Spirit. Some now suggest that, although the previous story is entertaining, it is not accurate, as Columbus had predetermined the name of the island before setting sail on his third voyage.[6]

Upon encountering the indigenous people of Trinidad, the Spanish routinely described the Arawaks as "friendly" and "peaceful," while the Caribs, who regularly fought against the Spanish, were labeled "cannibals" and "savages." As we will see, these distinctions often served various socio-political and economic agendas.

Regardless of whether they were considered friend or foe, over the next few hundred years, most of the indigenous population would be decimated, murdered by the Spanish and killed by diseases brought by the Europeans to which they

---

[5] Ian Lambie, "Inaccuracies about TT Emblems," *Trinidad and Tobago Newsday*, September 3, 2014, accessed August 16, 2015, http://newsday.co.tt/commentary/0,199944.html. An alternate spelling of "kairi" is "cayri." See Cristo Adonis and Jo-Anne S. Ferreira, "Amerindian Languages in Trinidad and Tobago," *St. Augustine News*, UWI Marketing and Communications Office, accessed August 16, 2015, http://sta.uwi.edu/stan/article13.asp.

[6] Ian Lambie, "Correcting history of Columbus in Trinidad," *Trinidad Guardian Online*, July 14, 2013, accessed August 16, 2015, http://www.guardian.co.tt/letters/2013-06-13/correcting-history-columbus-trinidad. For an interesting discussion of how Columbus created various toponyms, see Evelina Gužauskytė, *Christopher Columbus's Naming in the 'diarios' of the Four Voyages* (1492-1504): *A Discourse of Negotiation* (Toronto, Buffalo, London: University of Toronto Press, 2014).

had no immunity. Those who survived were subjugated by the Spanish, who compelled them to convert to Christianity and to labor on the *encomiendas*.

> The *encomienda* system was created by the Spanish to control and regulate American Indian labor and behavior during the colonization of the Americas. Under the *encomienda* system, conquistadors and other leaders (encomenderos) received grants of a number of Indians, from whom they could exact "tribute" in the form of gold or labor. The *encomenderos* were supposed to protect and Christianize the Indians granted to them, but they most often used the system to effectively enslave the Indians and take their lands.[7]

Some indigenous people were forced into slavery outright, and many were sold as slaves throughout the Americas. A 1503 decree made by Queen Isabella of Spain permitted Amerindians who were "cannibals" to be sold into slavery throughout the Spanish Empire. This essentially gave the Spanish permission to subjugate the "war-like" Caribs, who had been resisting Spanish colonization of the land, and who, conveniently, had been branded as cannibals. However, the result of Isabella's decree was that many Amerindians were erroneously labeled as Caribs, so that they might be sold into slavery. In addition, a 1511 Cédula declared Trinidad to be a "Carib" nation, "under pressure from the colonists of Santo Domingo for an increased labour force."[8] Scholar Neil Whitehead suggests that a reversal of the 1511 Cédula in 1518 was due not only to the efforts of Bartolomé de las Ca-

[7] "Ecomienda system established," *The Gilder Lehrman Institute of American History*, The Gilder Lehrman Institute of American History, accessed August 16, 2015, http://www.gilderlehrman.org/history-by-era/imperial-rivalries/timeline-terms/encomienda-system-established.

[8] Neil Whitehead, "Carib cannibalism. The historical evidence," *Journal de la Société des Américanistes*, Tome 70 (1984), 71.

sas on behalf of indigenous people in the Americas, but also because of increasing reports of gold in Trinidad and a desire to maintain the "native labour force."[9]

During one of our many trips to Trinidad as children, David and I were taken to the Botanic Gardens in Port of Spain, where we somehow got separated from my brother's godmother, Aunty Claire. And within that space of time, we came upon an Amerindian warrior. There was anger in his face. He carried a bow and arrow, which he pointed at us. We ran. David doesn't remember, but he was there. I sometimes think about this warrior. I can imagine he was protecting himself and his people from those who eventually caused their demise. I wonder if he is still there, caught between this world and the next. Or maybe all time and space exist simultaneously, and as kids my brother and I were able to pierce the veil that separates us.

With a large percentage of the indigenous population eradicated, and Spain preoccupied with its other territories, Trinidad would remain sparsely populated until the late eighteenth century. In 1783, a *Cédula de población* was implemented in an effort to populate the island. This decree gave permission to non-Spanish Catholics to settle land in Trinidad in exchange for loyalty to Spain. The result was that a significant number of French planters migrated to the island with their African slaves.

French planters living in the Americas had good reason to migrate to Trinidad and elsewhere in the region. The late 1700s saw a lot of unrest in the world that had serious implications for the Americas in general, and for the French in particular. The United States declared its independence in 1776, and within a decade the French Revolution had commenced (1787-1799). As the French were engaged in battle on their own soil, the Haitian Revolution erupted (1791-1804), and Haiti eventually became the second country in the New World (the first being the U.S.) to successfully fight for and gain its independence. Perhaps more significantly, Haiti be-

---

[9] Ibid.

came the first independent black nation in the New World. As a result of the unrest in France and Haiti, France's largest and most lucrative colony, many French planters left colonies in the French Caribbean (including places like Martinique and Guadeloupe) and sought refuge in Trinidad and elsewhere in the Americas.[10]

The British Takeover

Oh, Abercomby[11] sailed the sea,
With Harvey at his side,
Until they came to Trinity,
Upon the weltering tide,
They sailed in at the Dragon's Mouth,
By Madam Teteron's Rock-a,
And there in Chaguaramas Bay,
They came on Apodocca.

Oh, Apodocca sleeps so sound,
Who'll waken Apodocca?
—"The Lament for Apodocca," A.D. Russell[12]

I once came home after doing some research on the early history of Trinidad, and my mother gleefully began reciting "The Lament for Apodocca." She didn't recite the entire thing, just enough for me to get the gist of how the Spanish lost Trinidad to the British. As alluded to in the poem, in 1797, Rear Admiral Sebastián Ruiz de Apodaca,[13] the Spanish admiral

---

[10] A significant number of French planters from Haiti relocated to Cuba and New Orleans with their slaves.

[11] Sir Ralph Abercromby. His name is misspelled in the poem.

[12] Alexander David Russell, *Legends of the Bocas, Trinidad* (London: Oakley House, 1922), 81.

[13] Apodaca's name is misspelled in Russell's poem.

tasked with guarding the island of Trinidad, found himself severely outnumbered by the British fleet. Instead of fighting, the admiral decided to burn his ships and surrender. Thus, the British captured the island of Trinidad without much fanfare. The poem, written by a Brit, erroneously (and somewhat comically) asserts that "Apodocca" killed himself by going down with his ship.[14]

In 1802, four years after its capture, Trinidad was formally ceded to the British. Descriptions of the ensuing years frequently depict Trinidad as being a British colony with Spanish laws and an Afro-French culture. Following the implementation of the 1783 *Cédula de población*, and the importation of enslaved Africans to the island, Trinidad quickly became a plantation economy. However, the institution of slavery within that context was relatively short-lived in Trinidad, especially when compared with other Caribbean islands. This is not to say that slavery in Trinidad was not cruel, because it surely was. The British slave trade was outlawed in 1807, and less than half a century after the island's capitulation to the British, slavery was abolished in Trinidad. Emancipation was formally granted on August 1, 1838.

For former slave owners, survival hinged on the still-lucrative plantation economy, and in the absence of slave labor, a new exploitive system—indentured servitude—was developed. For the most part, these laborers came from China, India, and West Africa. The first set of laborers consisted of Chinese workers who arrived in Trinidad in 1806, shortly before the abolition of the slave trade in 1807. During the colonial era, they continued arriving in small numbers in periodic waves until the start of the Chinese Revolution in 1949.[15] And from 1841-1867, approximately 8,300-9,000 free Africans arrived in Trinidad, helping to reinvigorate African culture in

---

[14] Ibid., 82. "She sinks, her Admiral sinks with her, / He's flung his life away.... / Now he sleeps sound (as he was wont), / In Chaguaramus Bay!"

[15] See Walton Look Lai, *The Chinese in the West Indies, 1806-1995: A Documentary History*, (Kingston: University Press of the West Indies, 1998).

the island.[16] However, numerically speaking, the most significant of those who came to Trinidad to work during the post-Emancipation era were Indians, or East Indians as they are called locally. In 1845, the first wave of East Indians arrived in Trinidad, and as noted previously, they are currently the largest ethnic group in the nation.

Further adding to the diversity of the island were the *cocoa payols*, Venezuelan peons who migrated to Trinidad during the nineteenth century to work on the cocoa plantations,[17] as well as ethnic Syrians and Lebanese who, around the turn of the twentieth century, migrated to Trinidad, escaping religious persecution in their homelands. And adding to the callaloo pot were migrants from other (mostly British) Caribbean islands who, like my ancestors before me, traveled to Trinidad seeking employment and a better life.[18]

The Road to Independence

Cue: "Federation," "Our Model Nation," Mighty Sparrow

By the middle of the twentieth century, Britain was releasing its grip on its former colonies, and many of them were heading towards self-rule. In the Caribbean, many of Britain's colonies were in the process of forming a unified government known as the "West Indies Federation." However, the fledgling

---

[16] See Kenneth Anthony Lum, *Praising His Name in the Dance: Spirit Possession in the Spiritual Baptist Faith and Orisha Work in Trinidad, West Indies* (Newark: Hardwood Academic Publishers, 2000), 200, and Ryan Bazinet, "Shango Dance Across the Water: Music and the Re-Construction of Trinidadian," in "Orisha in New York City," *Re-constructing Place and Space: Media, Culture, Discourse and the Constitution of Caribbean Diasporas*, ed. Kamille Gentles-Peart and Maurice L. Hall, (Newcastle upon Tyne: Cambridge Scholars Publishing, 2012), 127.

[17] *Cocoa panyols* is an alternate spelling. Both *payol* and *panyol* are creolizations of the word *español*, which means Spanish. These payols contributed to the local culture most notably by helping to maintain a Spanish musical tradition known as parang.

[18] Trinidad is still a destination for many Caribbean migrants seeking employment opportunities.

federation was not to be. Jamaica eventually pulled out, and the union subsequently disintegrated. I would learn of its demise through another one of Sparrow's songs ("Federation") that my mother would sing. Looking straight at me and using her pointer finger to emphasize certain words, she sang:

If they [Jamaica] know they didn't want Federation (Federation)
And if they know they didn't want to unite as one (And only one)
I said to tell the Doctor [Eric Williams] you not in favor
Don't behave like a blasted traitor
This is no time to say you ent federating no more[19]

Despite the unsuccessful launch of the West Indies Federation, Britain's former colonies began acquiring their independence in rapid succession. Jamaica was the first, becoming independent on August 6, 1962, with Trinidad and Tobago following suit on on August 31st of that year. Trinidad's national anthem would be a recycled version of the anthem written for the West Indies Federation by Patrick Castagne. Nonetheless, it would capture the essence of the new nation and reflect its diverse history, as the last two stanzas of the song suggest.

Side by side we stand
Islands of the blue Caribbean Sea
This our native land
We pledge our lives to thee
Here every creed and race
Find an equal place
And may God bless our nation

Yes. May God bless our sweet, sweet TnT.

---

[19] My mother's rendition of the song's chorus differs somewhat (but not significantly) from the original recording.

Diego Martin

That first trip to Trinidad was also my first trip in an airplane. "*Pan Am!*" I can hear the words of the now defunct airline being sung in an advertisement. Our journey began at John F. Kennedy International Airport (JFK), where we retrieved our tickets and made our way to the baggage screening. In those days, you could travel with a lot of luggage *free of charge*, and we did. We would be gone for the entire summer and Mom packed a lot of things for the journey. We had boxes of food. Mom wasn't sure we'd like some of the food in Trinidad, and so she packed pasta and tomato sauce, Tang, and our favorite cereals.

During that first trip to Trinidad, I never thought too much about Aunty Elaine. It never occurred to me that she had only recently passed away. If there was a void, I never sensed it. When we arrived at the house in Diego Martin, in the northwestern part of the island, Aunty Ruby was there waiting for us with open arms. David ran to her, perhaps at my mom's urging, and gave her a big hug. All I could think was, "Who's this crazy lady David is running to?"

Aunty Ruby was my grandmother's older sister, the second of three children born to Florence "Mercy" Dixon and O'Connell Felix, or "Papa," as he was called. It would appear that we come from a line of threes, at least on my maternal grandmother's side of the family. Mercy Dixon was the youngest of three sisters from Tobago. She was considerably younger than her sisters, and it seems that they didn't always treat her kindly. They may have even resented her.

All three sisters married. One married a Park, one married a Bedlow, and one (my great-grandmother) married a Felix. Papa's French last name reflects Trinidad's French heritage. His father, Jean Camille Felix, was from Dominica, and it seems that he was an orphan who grew up with Catholic priests. Word has it that he never married Papa's mother, who was from Barbados.

My great-grandmother had many pregnancies but suffered almost as many miscarriages. She did have one child born after Grandma, Norma, but she died shortly after birth. Apparently, as a result of her frequent miscarriages, my great-grandmother had been sickly for many years, and she eventually died when my grandmother was just fourteen years old. However, her death seems to have been the result of medical negligence. Experiencing pain after having surgery, she was taken to the hospital where it was determined that gauze, needles, and other "stuff" had been left in her body. These foreign objects were subsequently removed; however, she never recovered.

I was sad to learn that my great-grandfather, Papa, was not very nice to my great-grandmother, or to my grandmother and her sisters, for that matter. After their mother died, Papa left his daughters to go live with his mistress—"the Indian woman." He even sold the plot where my great-grandmother was buried. He eventually returned to his children when he began losing his eyesight due to what were likely cataracts. And because Papa was born before surgical interventions for cataracts were commonplace, he would become fully blind and need the assistance of the very family he once neglected.

Grandma and Aunty Ruby really didn't think it was their responsibility to look after their father, especially after he had abandoned them. But Aunty Elaine insisted. And those of you who think that he wasn't adequately punished for his past misdeeds may find some consolation in the fact that two of Aunty Elaine's three children—Frankie and Lourdelle—used to take advantage of their grandfather's impaired vision by stealing the meat out of the food that Aunty Elaine would have them deliver to him, until one day he asked, "Elaine, yuh don't put meat in the food?"

After he went blind, Papa went to live in the house in Diego Martin, in the home where my brother and I would stay for most of the summer when we traveled to Trinidad. Aunty Ruby had purchased the home in 1955; it was one of the many newly constructed homes in the area. She moved in with her infant son, Bryan, and her elder sister—Aunty Elaine—and her family. Although technically the house belonged to Aunty Ruby, Aunty Elaine ran the place. She was the homemaker and, in essence, the matriarch. To my knowledge, the house in Diego Martin has not changed too much since the first generation of my family lived there. The greatest change over the years has been an addition that was already in place by the time David and I made our first trip.

The house, situated at the end of a short cul-de-sac just off the Diego Martin Main Road, is one of seven dwellings on the street. As you walk up the block, each side of the street is flanked with modest homes, most of which were bought by our neighbors around the same time that Aunty Ruby bought hers. At the end of the road stand two houses, each gated at the front and separated by another gate that runs from the street to the back of the property. The house on the left belongs to my family.

Along the right side of the house is a huge yard where David and I—city kids— spent whole days exploring the treasures to be found in a more natural habitat. We soon discovered all manner of flora and fauna. Over the years, an assortment of plants and fruits had thrived in the yard. At one point, there was a cherry tree and a guava tree that I once got stuck in while playing hide and seek. As I got older, it seemed like the vegetation in the yard only grew. Avocado, paw-paw (papaya), sapodilla, sorrel, and lemongrass all grew in the yard. At one point, Aunty Ruby's son, Bryan, even planted a noni tree. He probably did so during the early 2000s, when the fruit of the noni tree became widely popular for its medicinal properties.

Cue: "Mangoes," Trinidad Folksong

The one thing we didn't have was a mango tree. But that was okay; there are so many mango trees on the island that when the fruit is in season family and friends are bound to give you some from their own trees. As an American, it never ceases to amaze me just how many varieties of mangoes exist. To this day, I can still only recognize a handful. My parents can go on for days listing mango types. My mom would often sing a line from a popular calypso—"I want a penny to buy mango vert, mango teen"—before rattling off a list of mangoes: *mango vert*, mango teen, *dou-douce mango*, Julie mango, etc.[20]

Life was simple then, and it's only as I got older that I realized the profundity of simple living. Our time in Trinidad would stand in stark contrast to life in the United States and especially in New York City. In the mornings, David and I would wake up and brush our teeth with pure baking soda, and we hated it. (Years later, when tooth manufacturers began putting baking soda in toothpastes, I laughed at how so-called "third-world" folk already knew the benefits of the household item for oral hygiene.) Then, we'd have breakfast, most likely some cereal brought from home, but we'd also be offered "tea," which turned out to be hot chocolate (which I hated), and biscuit, which to my surprise was not a cookie but rather a piece of dry Crix.[21]

After breakfast, we'd play for most of the day—hide and seek, tag, redlight/greenlight 1-2-3. We'd even pretend we were Kung Fu masters as we play-fought with our cousins. We also spent time exploring the living creatures of the island. David took a liking to the lizards. Prior to our first trip, we'd never seen a lizard before, at least not in person. We'd seen cockroaches, and rats the size of cats in the subways of New York City, but a lizard, that was a new experience. I wasn't a fan, but David liked to chase them. He'd run behind one before seizing it. No sooner than he thought the creature was secure in his hands, it would separate its tail from the rest of its body and quickly crawl away. The tail would remain in my brother's hands until he dropped it, and it would continue writhing and wiggling, as though it had a life of its own.

The house in Diego Martin was bigger than our New York apartment, and in many ways, Trinidad became a summer haven for my brother and me. Brooklyn during the 1980s wasn't

---

[20] Rose mango, starch mango, calabash mango, soursop mango, table mango, grafted mango…

[21] A type of cracker.

exactly the safest place to be. Besides, when we lived in the apartment on E. 54th Street, my parents didn't allow us to play on the sidewalks. In Trinidad, we were free to roam and discover an environment that offered more than concrete, cockroaches, and rodents.

The Yard

During her childhood, my mom spent a significant amount of time living with her aunts and extended family in Diego Martin. The rest of the time, she lived with her parents and younger brother in a *yard* in one of the more impoverished areas of Port of Spain, the capital. I've never been to a yard, but on countless occasions, my mother has described the one she lived in on Prescott Alley[22] in East Dry River. Two generations of my family lived there—my grandmother and her sisters, and later my mom, uncle, and grandparents. I'm not sure why my brother and I never visited Prescott Alley as children, but by the time I was old enough to do so on my own, I was told that it was too dangerous, especially for outsiders; it's not an area where people should go unless they live there or are accompanied by someone who does. Nonetheless, my mother's life growing up in Trinidad has always seemed idyllic to me, even if by American standards her living conditions were anything but.

Historically, the yard—an abbreviation for the term *barrack-yard*—and the areas in which they are located have generally been places of poverty and ill-repute. An article in the *Trinidad and Tobago Newsday* states that "under section 134, sub-section 2 of the Public Health Ordinance, a barrack yard was defined as 'any building or collection of buildings divided into rooms occupied singly or in sets by persons of the poorer classes, and to which there are a common barrack-yard and

[22] For years, I did not know that the place where my mom had lived was called "Prescott Alley," as the pronunciation sounded to me like one word: "PRES-CAH-TAL-EE."

common conveniences.'"[23] Trinidadian writer and activist C.L.R. James paints a more colorful picture of the barrack-yard in his short story "Triumph," published in 1929—the year after my grandmother was born.

> Where people in England and America say slums, Trinidadians speak of barrack-yards. Probably the word is a relic of the days when England relied as much on garrisons of soldiers as on her fleet to protect her valuable sugar-producing colonies. Every street in Port of Spain proper can show you numerous examples of the type: a narrow gateway leading into a fairly big yard, on either side of which run long low buildings, consisting of anything from four to eighteen rooms, each about twelve feet square. In these live, and have always lived, the porters, prostitutes, carter-men, washerwomen, and domestic servants of the city.
>
> In one corner of the yard is the hopelessly inadequate water-closet, unmistakable to the nose if not to the eye; sometimes there is a structure with the title of bathroom: a courtesy title, for he or she who would wash in it with decent privacy must cover the person as if bathing on the Lido; the kitchen happily presents no difficulty: never is there one and each barrack-yarder cooks before her door. In the centre of the yard is a heap of stones. On these half-laundered clothes are bleached before being finally spread out to dry on the wire lines which in every yard cross and recross each other in all directions.[24]

---

[23] Carol Matroo, "Barrack Yard to Back Stage," *Trinidad and Tobago Newsday*, February 19, 2012, accessed August 16, 2015, http://www.newsday.co.tt/carnival_2012/0,155631.html.

[24] C.L.R. James, "Triumph," in *The C.L.R. James Reader*, ed. Anna Grimshaw (Oxford and Cambridge: Blackwell, 1992), 29.

Much of his description rings true with what I've been told about my family's past. My great-grandmother, Mercy, was a cook who worked out of her home. Papa was, as my mother would say, "a carpenter by day and a musician by night." And according to my mom, her home in Prescott Alley was essentially a one-room apartment until the people in the adjacent apartment left, and her parents quickly took over that one by breaking down the wood partition that separated the two households. As James suggests, privacy was scarce. But for me, the real kicker was that there was only one toilet in the yard, and it was shared among *all* its residents. Now the "potty," or chamber pot, that my grandmother kept, even when we had two bathrooms in the house, made perfect sense.

Despite the poverty that existed in the yard, it was nonetheless a place where creativity thrived. As we will see, it was in the barrack-yards of the eastern sections of Port of Spain that some of Trinidad's most revered artistic traditions were developed, many of which became a crucial part of Trinidad's celebration par excellence—carnival.

Dem Small Islanders

Cue: "Trinidad the Godfather," King Swallow

As mentioned earlier, my mother would divide her time between Prescott Alley and the house in Diego Martin, essentially living with Aunty Elaine, her husband, Uncle Carl, and their three children—Frankie, Lourdelle, and "Pinky." Now, Uncle Carl was from Barbados, although I was grown before I had become aware of that fact.

"How you could think Carl was from Trinidad?" my mother asked, somewhat annoyed. "Carl talk like a real Bajan," she continued.

Well, for me, Uncle Carl was just Uncle Carl. I have fond memories of him sitting in his leather recliner, smoking a pipe or reading a newspaper. During those summer trips to Trinidad, my brother and I didn't see too much of him during the day. Uncle Carl would go for long walks. He'd set off during the morning, return home for lunch, and then leave again. He'd finally make his way back home during the evening.

I never once thought of Uncle Carl as a man with an accent that distinguished him from the rest of the household. His accent certainly wasn't as strong as Aunty Elita's, who was also from Barbados and one of my mom's many pen pals. Once she came to visit us in our home in Brooklyn, and her manner of speaking struck me as odd. I was in another room when I heard her talking to my mom about a "boy-cicle."

"Boy…boy-cicle." I repeated over and over to myself, trying to make sense of what I had heard.

Finally I thought, "Bicycle! Does she mean bicycle?!"[25]

Uncle Carl's speech never made me scratch my head or question my hearing. His familiar calling of "Dani…Dan-Dan" had no accent per se. It was just Uncle Carl calling my name in his inimitable way. I figured I was in Trinidad, so everyone was Trinidadian. Besides, I wasn't really concerned with where he was from anyway.

Nonetheless, "small islanders" have not gone unrecognized by Trinidadians, partly because many Trinidadians can trace their roots to the various "small islands" of the Caribbean. King Swallow,[26] a calypsonian from Antigua, even sang a song in which he refers to Trinidad as the "Caribbean Godfather" who welcomes to the island his godchildren, "small islanders" who have migrated seeking a better living in the oil-rich country. Nonetheless, small islanders have at times been met with animosity and/or ridicule in Trinidad.

Cue: "Take Yuh Meat Out Muh Rice," "Kaka Roach," Lord Kitchener

Fan favorite Lord Kitchener has two calypsos that humorously address his encounter with two small islanders—a Bajan and a Grenadian. In "Take Yuh Meat Out Muh Rice," Kitch tells the story of a slick Bajan who inveigles him to contribute

[25] This foreshadowed the "grennid" incident with my dad.

[26] He is also known as the "Mighty Swallow."

his meat to a pot of rice cooked by the Bajan. After the food is cooked, the Bajan tells Kitch:

Trini, I'm a born Barbadian
I don't like to fight
But when come to the occasion
Man I stick for meh right
You put in a twelve cents meat bone
You worse than a lice
I goin' give you a word of advice
Take yuh meat out muh rice!

The cost of the meat bone decreases with each subsequent chorus—ten cents, nine cents, and finally eight cents. Much of the humor derives from the way that the Bajan swindles the Trini, especially as Trinidadians are considered to be tricksters.[27] But the song is just as humorous, if not more so, because of Kitch's imitation of Bajan speech, which is perhaps among the most distinct in the Anglophone Caribbean.

In another song, "Kaka Roach," Kitchener describes a Grenadian who becomes the source of mockery by Trinidadians on carnival day after she uses the word "kaka roach" instead of "cockroach" when complaining about her filthy apartment and "slumlord."

The Grenadian vex like hell
'Til she start to blow,
"Trinidad people want foo make me a pappy show
Whether it's kaka roach, cockroach or kakaree
Well, most important everybody know what I mean"

Despite her protests, the Grenadian's words of "kaka roach in me petticoat" are turned into a *lavway*[28] sung by carnival revelers. Leave it to Trinis to turn anything into fodder for carnival.

---

[27] Remember we talked about those "Trickidadians"?

[28] From the French *la voix*, meaning "the voice," a lavway is the chorus (or response) used in a call and response song.

* * *

So far, I haven't really said too much about carnival, and maybe it's about time that I do. Truthfully, my parents weren't so big into carnival, at least in the sense that they did not play mas'.[29] But my father's mother, Grandma Helen, was once Queen of a carnival band. She liked to play her mas', but somehow it didn't rub off on my dad. Although his mother would make him play "kiddie mas'" as child, he didn't like it too much. The Christian calling had already infected his blood, even if he would not become aware of the fact until much later.

Perhaps he was immune to the carnival fever, but I was surely afflicted time and time again. Like my mother, I liked a bit of bacchanal. Although I would not experience a carnival until I was well into my twenties, it was always vivid in my mind. My mother's memories of carnival became my own. Coupled with the music of carnival that every year flooded the streets of East Flatbush and the other neighboring West Indian communities in Brooklyn, her stories help me to create memories of a celebration that I had yet to attend in body. I could see the lavish costumes—imagined by mas' designers who showed off their brilliant minds, and made real by those who would don them. I could see, too, all those Trinidadians who faithfully came out in numbers to the mas' camps where night and day they would bend wire, sew beads, and glue feathers so that the people's costumes would be ready on time.

I admire their skill and dedication, but mas' making wasn't my thing. Though, at my mother's suggestion, I did once play a red devil in elementary school—*Jab! Jab!*—and I once designed and constructed a butterfly costume for my younger sister when she was a child. But my foray into carnival was largely through the music, the sounds that carried the rhythms and messages of our people for generations. It was this music that helped make Trinidad carnival "the greatest show on Earth." My mother would say that "no other carnival could

[29] The term mas' is an abbreviation of the word masquerade, and to "play mas'" refers to dressing in costume and masquerading (or masking) during carnival.

touch we carnival," and by the way that it has been mass-produced across the globe, she just may be right.

The Greatest Show on Earth

Cue: "Rainorama," Lord Kitchener

My mother's second to last carnival almost didn't happen. In 1972, a polio epidemic forced the cancellation of the official dates of carnival—the Monday and Tuesday before Lent. Instead, carnival was held later, on May first and second of that year. The event was later immortalized in Kitchener's song, "Rainorama," where the calypsonian presents a vivid picture of the events surrounding the cancellation of carnival, as well as the elation of revelers once the celebration was rescheduled.

And they start to jump around! (Yah!)
And they start to tumble down! (Yah!)
And they fall down on the ground! (Yah!)
If you see how they gay!
But what was so comical,
In the midst of bacchanal
Rain come and wash out mas' in May!

Kitchener's song makes explicit the importance of the centuries-old tradition for Trinidadians.

Like in other parts of the Americas, the staging of pre-Lenten carnivals was brought to Trinidad by Europeans. However, enslaved and free Africans incorporated various African musical and carnivalesque traditions into a European framework.[30]

Cue: "When Ah Dead Bury Meh Clothes," Growling Tiger; "Stick Fight," Anslem Douglas; "Mastife," "Calypso," David Rudder; "De Trini Way," Destra Garcia; "Dead or Alive," Shurwayne Winchester

---

[30] Trinidad's carnival traditions largely reflect an Afro-French ethos.

It happened one night while walking through the town of Woodbrook in Port of Spain. I heard a sudden rumbling of drums; it sounded like the earth was shaking. Then, I saw the faint glow of a flambeau in the distance.

"Canboulay," I thought, somewhat relieved.

In Trinidad, enslaved Africans were tasked with extinguishing cane fires that erupted spontaneously or that were set surreptitiously by the slaves themselves.

> At the time of a plantation fire, *bandes* from different estates, each with its whip-carrying slave driver, were assembled, by the blaring of horns, to deal with the emergency. The *negre jardins* (or field slaves), who comprised the *bandes*, carried torches (for night-time illumination) and drums (for rhythmic accompaniment to their work songs). 'In such cases', recalled 'X' in the *Port of Spain Gazette* in 1881, 'the gangs of the neighbouring Estates proceeded alternately, accompanied with torches at night, to the Estate which had suffered, to assist in grinding the burnt canes before they became sour. The work went on night and day until all the canes were manufactured into sugar.'[31]

Upon being emancipated, former slaves reenacted the putting out of cane fires as a form of celebration, and thus emerged the canboulay, a word derived from the French *cannes brûlées*, or "burnt cane." Essentially an African form of street procession, the canboulay eventually found its way into the carnival. Incorporating several artistic expressions that can be (and often are) performed independently, the canboulay has contributed substantially to Trinidad's carnival celebrations. Group processions, African-styled masquerades, and stickfighting—with their drumming and call and response singing—are all aspects of the canboulay that continue as vital aspects of car-

---

[31] John Cowley, *Carnival, Canboulay and Calypso: Traditions in the Making* (Cambridge: Cambridge University Press, 1998), 20.

nival and Trinidad culture in general.

As I listened to the drums and the chant of the chorus, moving ever so closer to me, I couldn't help but imagine the fear of the plantation owners, whose livelihood depended upon African bodies extinguishing the fires that ravaged the very crops they were forced to cultivate.

The drum was a force to be reckoned with, and so in Trinidad—in fact, wherever black people had been brought as slaves—they were at some point banned. You see, the drum was a troublemaker. Like the serpent talking to Eve, the drum talked to the people, enslaved Africans, making them want to revolt. In many West African and Central African societies, from whence most of the enslaved Africans in the Americas originated, drums were and are a method of communication. They were a direct link to God, the orishas, ancestors, and the living. They mimicked the tonal inflections of speech, and so when brought to the Americas, the enslaved used drums to talk to each other in preparation for rebellions and revolts. However, European colonizers and slave owners eventually recognized (though did not necessarily understand) the power of the drum and swiftly banned its practice.

In Trinidad, the drums also had been used to accompany the *batonniers*, or stickfighters, who challenged each other to bloody duels. Each batonnier belonged to a group that had not only fighters, but also musicians. The drummers were important, but equally, if not more so, were the *chantwells*,[32] singers who were tasked with encouraging their bands of fighters while lambasting their rivals'. A chorus would respond to the chantwell's call with a lively lavway. And from the chantwell would emerge the calypsonian.

They say necessity is the mother of invention, so when drumming was banned in Trinidad in the 1880s, the people

[32] From the French word *chantuelle*, meaning "singer."

birthed a new creation—*tamboo bamboo*.[33] This collection of instruments, made from bamboo cut into various sizes, produced sound when musicians pounded the different sized pieces on the ground, creating several pitches. And just as the rhythms of the drum were reinterpreted on the tamboo bamboo, the rhythms of the tamboo bamboo would later be reinterpreted on what would eventually become the national instrument of Trinidad and Tobago—the steelpan.

I see a people creative who must overcome
Make magic from old steel, from rusty old drum
—"Nah Leaving," Denyse Plummer

Cue: "The Road," Lord Kitchener; "Outcast," Mighty Sparrow; "Pan in 'A' Minor," Lord Kitchener; "Pan in 'A' Minor," Renegades Steel Orchestra; "The Hammer," David Rudder; "Calling Meh," Destra Garcia

Like I said before, my grandmother and her sisters were from a part of town that didn't have the best reputation. It was also one of the areas in which steelpan developed. Steelbands were a fixture in East Port of Spain, where those badjohns—panmen—would get into musical battles and physical ones too. *It was one set ah commess*[34] *in de place!* They had a penchant for fighting with each other and with the authorities who would try to seize and destroy their pans. These men, and the women who accompanied them, were considered ruffians, hooligans, thugs—the scourge of the island. They were so bad that Sparrow wrote a song about them. Mom would always sing a few choice lines:

---

[33] Ethnomusicologist Shannon Dudley states that "bamboo percussion was likely played in Trinidad prior to the 1880s," and that it "has precedents in many African and Caribbean cultures." However, the emergence of bamboo percussion in the carnival seems to be a direct result of the ban on drumming. Shannon Dudley, *Music from Behind the Bridge: Steelband Aesthetics and Politics in Trinidad and Tobago* (New York: Oxford University Press, 2008), 41.

[34] Commess means confusion.

If yuh sister talk to a steelband man
The family want to break she hand
Put she out, lick out every teeth in she mouth[35]

Kitch wrote about them too, and he pulled no punches letting all of Trinidad know that any disturbance of his carnival band by the fight-prone panmen would lead to disaster for them. Mom would sing to me how Kitch "hear how they plannin' for the carnival coming." How "they go beat people and they don't care 'bout trouble." But Kitch put them in their place, singing:

The road make to walk on carnival day
Constable, I don't want to talk but I got to say
Any steelband man only venture to break this band
Is a long funeral from the Royal Hospital[36]

By the time I was born, the steelbands had lost their violent reputation. Any battles between the bands were purely of a musical nature. The carnival festivities acquired a new, state-sanctioned pan battle known as Panorama, and Kitchener himself became a vocal supporter of the steelbands. His "Pan in 'A' Minor"—a classic, made more so by Jit Samaroo's iconic arrangement performed by the Amoco Renegades Steel Orchestra during the 1987 Panorama competition—is a sort of ode to the most popular steelbands and a challenge to their arrangers.

Boogsie on the tenor (Beat pan!)
Bringing out the minor (Beat pan!)
Up come "The Professor" (Beat pan!)
To add to the fire (Beat pan!)
I calling on Bradley (Beat pan!)
To challenge Beverly (Beat pan!)

---

[35] Mighty Sparrow, "Outcast."

[36] Lord Kitchener, "The Road."

Which means Desperado (Beat pan!)
Go answer Tokyo (Beat pan!)[37]

He reminds the arrangers that they are "fighting" in a new era, not physically, but "for tonal quality, the spirit of carnival, and good phrase."

Carnival is so much more than canboulay, calypso, and steelpan, but I have to stop somewhere, and here seems appropriate. Trinidad has many other cultural artforms, including one in particular that I took up to honor my father's paternal grandmother, Tantie Maggie.

Sangre Grande

I was fortunate to have met three of my father's grandparents. My favorite, if only because I spent the most quality time with her, was my great-grandmother, Margaret Bocage. Tantie Maggie, as we called her,[38] was my dad's paternal grandmother. She was a kind woman, and during our visits, I used to tag around her like a little puppy. I always felt connected to her, and that connection would remain even after she died.

Tantie Maggie lived in "Sandy Grandy." For years, I thought the town derived its name from its sandy streets and (in my mind) the abundance of old people living there. Turns out that "Sandy Grandy" was a nickname for "Sangre Grande," a Spanish term meaning "Big Blood." The descriptive name makes reference to the reddish color of the waters belonging to a large tributary of the Oropouche River that runs through the region. Sangre Grande stands in contrast to "Sangre Chiquito," or "Little

---

[37] Lennox (Len) "Boogsie" Sharpe, Ken "Professor" Philmore, the late Clive Bradley, and Beverly Griffith are the names of popular arrangers in Trinidad. Desperadoes, or "Despers," and Tokyo refer to two steelbands.

[38] We also called her Aunty Maggie. "Tantie" is term of endearment and sign of respect that is often bestowed upon older women. It comes from the French word for aunt, *(la) tante*.

Blood," a nearby smaller tributary.[39] But to me, "Grandy" will always be the place with sand and grandfolks.

I was fascinated by Aunty Maggie and that side of the family, in part because they were visible reminders of an oft-forgotten past. Aunty Maggie and her siblings could be classified as "Spanish"—a local term in Trinidad that refers to people of mixed Spanish and Amerindian heritage. It was often used to describe people who looked "Spanish" rather than those who could actually claim "Spanish" ancestry. Many of the "Spanish" in Trinidad were cocoa payols. Others were descendants of Amerindians and Spaniards who had lived or settled in Trinidad. I'm not sure from what kind of "Spanish" I'm descended. Perhaps both, especially considering how much both Spaniards and Amerindians migrated between Trinidad and Venezuela. It seems somewhat arbitrary to assign a nationality. Anyway, Aunty Maggie died before I could ask her about her parents, and my grandfather—her son—could provide few details about his grandparents.

Apparently, Grandpa's maternal grandmother used to cuss in Spanish. The only other detail I recall him giving me about her was that no one could give my grandfather licks when she was around. My great-great-grandmother loved her grandson and likely spoiled him. My great-great-grandfather was a dark-skinned man, and unlike my great-great-grandmother, he would punish my grandfather when he misbehaved, one time making him grate coconuts.[40] My great-greats had seven children, including Aunty Maggie, and the genes in that family were clearly strong.

Catu was one of Aunty Maggie's sisters. She was short with long, straight black hair, and I always thought she looked like an indigenous person from the Peruvian Andes. I have vague memories of her house, but I clearly remember that she had a

[39] Michael Anthony, "Towns and Villages: Sangre Chiquito," *Trinidad and Tobago NALIS*, 2007, accessed August 16, 2015, http://www.nalis.gov.tt/Research/SubjectGuide/TownsandVillages/TownsandVillagesSZ/tabid/172/Default.aspx?PageContentID=155.

[40] That might be worse than a cuttail.

swinging bench in the front of her home that David and I enjoyed utilizing. She also had lots of cats. Grandpa filled in some more details about Catu when he mentioned that she used to keep a bucket filled with water in her kitchen. After visiting her home on several occasions, he began to notice that the water in the bucket always remained at the same level. Becoming curious, he lifted the bucket up and found that his aunt had money stashed underneath. That's all I know about Catu.

Petite (pronounced PEE-TEE) was the only other one of Aunty Maggie's siblings that I had had the opportunity to meet. She looked a lot like Aunty Maggie. They had the same slim build, and their African and "Spanish" heritages were juxtaposed on their faces. Wearing brown complexions and kinky hair (but not as kinky as mine), their faces sported high, indigenous cheekbones. On first sight, they perhaps looked very unlike their sisters Catu and Malcoline. (Mom said Malcoline looked even more "Spanish" than Catu.) And while Catu had cats, Petite had dogs—big dogs. The first time I ever saw a Great Dane was when I was in Trinidad visiting Petite. She had at least two, possibly more, and they were contained in a large kennel. They were gigantic, definitely taller than my five-year old self, and probably taller than my adult self. That's all I recalled of Petite until my grandfather planted a new memory in my head about how she once saved his life, but I'll save that for later.

I often wish that I were able to tap the knowledge of my great-grandmother and her generation. There's so much information that was never passed on. Apparently, Tantie Maggie spoke *patois*, the lingua franca in Trinidad throughout the nineteenth century and into the twentieth century. A primarily French-based patois incorporating African, English, and Spanish words, it is hardly spoken in Trinidad today. My grandfather once told me that he speaks it too, but when I asked him to say something in patois, he simply looked down and shook his head "no." I'm not sure why he wouldn't say anything, but I suspect that the language had started to slip from the recesses of his brain, if only from lack of use. But I digress.

I miss Tantie Maggie. Though I am certain that she watches over me from the beyond, I eventually sought to create a sense of closeness with her by becoming involved with a music associated with Trinidad's "Spanish" heritage.

Parang

Cue: "The Grinch," Myron B; "Caminante," Baron

One Christmas season, Aunty Maggie ran a group of *parranderos* from her house. I wasn't there, but my father had mentioned the event often enough for me to feel like I had been. Aunty Maggie had just finished polishing her vinyl floors when the rowdy group appeared at her home bringing Yuletide cheer and property destruction. The tradition of roving musicians serenading friends, family, and even strangers, especially during the Christmas season, is well known in Trinidad, even if it is little-known outside of the island. Parang, or *parranda*, as it is called in Spanish, refers to this act of merrymaking, and the music associated with it reflects Trinidad's colonial ties to Spain, as well as its historical relationship with neighboring Venezuela.

Cue: "Sereno, sereno," "A la medianoche," "Alegría," La Divina Pastora

Parang is sung mostly at Christmas time, obscuring the fact that not all parang is tied to the Christmas season and often prompting debates regarding whether the music is sacred or secular. Traditionally, the songs were sung in Spanish by groups of musicians—parranderos—who would travel by foot throughout the most rural parts of the island to the homes of family and friends to serenade them with an *aguinaldo*, or gift of song. In the old days (and sometimes today, though perhaps less frequently), parranderos used to show up to a home unannounced in the dead of night—one or two o'clock in the morning—when those inside were most likely to be asleep. In the distance, a light sleeper might hear the faint strumming of *cuatros* and guitars and the shaking of the *marac*.[41] Then, all of a sudden—*BOOM!* Everyone who has described to me the experience of being awoken by a parang side has likened it to an explosion of the most fantastic kind. Upon reaching their destination, the parranderos would strike up a *serenal*, or *levanta*, to wake up the residents inside and make them aware of the purpose for the visit.

Est[a] parrandita
Es de Siparia
Y venimos adorando
El hijo de Maria[42]

If the owners of the home were pleased, they would welcome the parranderos inside, where they would continue singing songs. If they weren't too pleased, they could a) pretend they're not at home or b) run the parang side from their door, Tantie Maggie style.

Traditionally, once inside of a home, the group continues singing songs in a particular order. First, they would sing songs based on the Christmas story, beginning with the *anunciación*, or Annunciation. As its name suggests, the Annunciation tells the story of the angel Gabriel's visit to the Virgin Mary to "announce" to her that she would give birth to the Messiah. Songs on the annunciation would be followed by songs on the *nacimiento*, or birth of Christ. These songs often emphasize Jesus' birth in a stable, surrounded by animals, and the subsequent visit by the Three Wise Men. Essentially, the nacimiento is a laudatory song in praise of the newly born baby Jesus.

After singing on the Christmas story, the parranderos sing a variety of secular songs. And at some point during the night, for all of their hard work, the parranderos are rewarded with

---

[41] Marac is an abbreviation of the word maracas. The term *shak shak* is also used as a synonym for a pair of maracas.

[42] La Divina Pastora, "Sereno, sereno." This little parang side / is from Siparia / And we come praising / Mary's son.

traditional Christmas fare—pastelles, ham, bread, black cake, ponche (de) crème, rum—or whatever the family had to offer.

Before leaving a home, the parranderos sing a *despedida*, or farewell song, in which they thank their hosts for their hospitality and wish them a Merry Christmas and a Happy New Year.

I'm not sure at what point Aunty Maggie tossed the hooligan parranderos from her home, but I am certain it was well before the despedida. It's doubtful that they even got through the anunciación because, from what I can tell, they were the epitome of the drunken parang side. You know, the kind that goes from house to house looking for food and whatever alcoholic drinks they can get their hands on—Puncheon, VAT, babash. Whatever damage they caused, it must have been substantial, because Aunty Maggie was among the kindest and most giving of people. She wouldn't throw people out of her house without cause.

I wish I could rewind time and go back to the days when Aunty Maggie was around, the days when my visits to Trinidad were truly idyllic, but like the wise Solomon once said, "to everything there is a season." Nothing in life is permanent.

Good Morning, Neighbor

Cue: "Good Mornin," 3 Canal (Pronounced TREE CA-NAL)

I was at the port, waiting in line to get on one of the high-speed boats that would take me from Port of Spain to Tobago.

"Good morning," I said to the attendant standing in front of me. She gave me what I thought to be a look of disgust, took my ticket, and then warmly greeted the white American couple behind me.

"From my own people," I thought to myself.

Maybe I should have spoken with an American accent. Maybe then she would have given me more respect. Maybe I should have stood taller, with my shoulders back. (I have a tendency to slouch.) Maybe I should have just been taller.

Maybe. Maybe. Maybe. Ugh.

I had only returned to Trinidad a few months prior, after too many years away. Our vacations in Trinidad were halted as my parents started sending us to Canada for the summer once Aunty Lourdelle, Pinky, and Uncle Carl had moved there in the 1990s. In 1998, during my freshman year in college, I was supposed to go to Trinidad for carnival. An English teacher had a course on carnival and had created a study abroad program. I wasn't in the class, but I received permission to go. When it appeared that I had not received any financial aid for the trip, my plans were abandoned. Later, I found out that I had received additional money from the school to participate in the program, but for some reason there was a miscommunication, and my mom was not immediately made aware of that fact.

Aunty Maggie died a few months after I was supposed to have traveled to Trinidad that year. I like to think that it was divine intervention that prevented me from going. I likely would have been caught in the midst of something that I would have been unable to handle. There were rumors. Rumors that she had been mistreated, perhaps killed, or left to die.

I eventually made it back to Trinidad in 2005, when I began an almost yearlong stay to conduct research for my dissertation on parang. It was during this time that I encountered the rude port attendant. In general, experiencing Trinidad as an adult was very different from experiencing the island as a child. For one, people didn't seem as friendly. At first I thought, "Maybe it's always been like this for adults. Maybe they've always only been nice to children." But I think that was wishful thinking on my part. The island had changed, and others had noticed too. People had changed, so much so that 3 Canal, a popular rapso group, sang a song about it—about the values that were being lost, about how Trinidadians could no longer manage to even greet their neighbors with a friendly "good morning."

What's going on? Please, tell me what's going on?
What's happening? Please, tell me what's happening?
Something gone wrong, like everything upside down, Lord!
Right now good [is] bad, is like this whole place gone mad
Everyday is a hustle and a bustle
Everybody right now caught in the jostle
For space in the race, trying to keep up the pace
But the space ram cram, everybody in a jam
Jamming, we jamming,
Jamming for a better life, a better way of living
In the mean time, simple things we forgetting
Like how to say, "Good morning."[43]

Saying "good morning" is one of those things you learn as a child along with "please" and "thank you." In West Indian culture (and many others as well) it is particularly disrespectful not to say good morning to people, or give them a proper greeting, particularly when entering their home. It seemed like common courtesies were slowly being eroded. How I wish the only problem was verbal amnesia, but I noticed more pressing issues.

One day, while riding in a maxi along the bus route, I sat looking out the window. I shuddered as we passed a decrepit cemetery. "No respect for the dead," I thought to myself. "This is why Trinidad is in the state that it's in." Another time, I found myself at the gravesite of one Aldwyn Roberts, better known as "Lord Kitchener." I felt honored to be standing at the resting place of one of my favorite calypsonians, one whose songs my mother often conjured up during my childhood. However, the litter strewn around the cemetery made me sick. Two of the most important aspects of African culture are respect for elders and respect for the dead. Although I didn't grow up making altars for my ancestors, some aspects of the culture surely seeped in.

---

[43] 3 Canal, "Good Mornin." For complete lyrics, see 3 Canal's official website, http://www.3canal.com/?section=music-4.

The island seemed to be increasingly Americanized (it full ah copycat!), and despite what some may think, to me the changes being made seemed to be the opposite of development and progress. I worry about Trinidad now. Like much of the world, Trinidad watches and follows the West closely, particularly the U.S., and I am afraid we are "gaining the world, and losing our souls." There is a strong and unhealthy desire for material things that has arguably led to an increase in crime, from kidnappings for ransom to *bobol*.[44] Some people blame the "barrel children," young people whose parents have emigrated but send expensive goods to their children who remain in Trinidad. Others blame return migrants, many of whom were deported to Trinidad after having been incarcerated for drugs and/or violent offenses. Then there are the government officials who care more about lining their pockets than making sure that the basic needs of all Trinidadians are met.

The situation is complex, but the root causes of what I would call degeneration instead of progress can be summed up in three words: bigger, better, faster. We want things that we perceive to be bigger, better, and faster, because we think these things add value to our lives. Unfortunately, this is a disease that I recognize all too well as a part of American society. It is the offspring of colonialism and imperialism. It is the new search for El Dorado, a desire for material positions so ardent that the destruction of Mother Earth, let alone the people on it, is considered collateral damage. This mentality has been infecting countries across the globe and increasingly creating economic disparities.

Perhaps the skyscrapers that keep expanding along the port in Trinidad's capital are an example of prosperity, but would we really block out the sun just to show that we could? The same progress that was built on the backs of indigenous, African, and Asian people in this land is now being built on the backs of the disenfranchised descendants of those same people. Our ancestors must be rolling in their graves.

---

[44] Bobol is a word used to describe to corruption.

Chapter 4:
Of God, Ghosts, and Obeah

If you call at midnight,
Jesus hear and he will answer
If you call at midnight,
The Holy Ghost set your soul on fire
The inspiration of the preacher
Send the sinner to the altar
Set he soul on fire
Blessed Holy Ghost, come down
Fall on Zion
—"Blessed Holy Ghost," Pentecostal Chorus

PART I: OF GOD

The Funeral

Cue: "Lorraine," Explainer

It had been almost five years since I had last touched down in the land of carnival, calypso, and steelpan—the land of my parents' birth. In my mind it felt like yesterday, but in my body I could feel age creeping in. There were a few reasons why I had stayed away, but much of it had to do with Grandpa and the stress that I'd felt even at the very thought of him. How ironic that my first trip in all these years would be to bury him.

As the plane began to taxi, the safety instructions for

Caribbean Airlines came into view on the many small television screens that dotted the aircraft. The sound of soca permeated the air. It seemed fitting that the song playing in the background was Explainer's "Lorraine." The airline played an instrumental version using a steelband, but I could hear the words in my head.

Lorraine, you bettah wake up
Ah need a jet plane to take me non-stop
Ah cyah stay in New York City
When there is sunshine and pan in my country,
Lions is the place with de jammin'
With Kalyan and Charlie's Roots clashin'
Everyone happy partyin'
And I'm freezin' in Brooklyn, Dahlin'!

Lorraine doh cry ah leavin'
Ah cyah miss dis jammin'
With all dem steelband beatin'
And woman background shakin'
If de bug bite you baby
Then you could come and join me
Inside Catelli steelband
Jammin' with some man woman

Yes. I was heading back home—to Trinidad. I had not expected to be returning under these circumstances, but I wasn't surprised by it. Grandpa had often made bad decisions for which other people had paid hefty prices, and I knew that I would eventually have to return to see that he received a proper burial.

Grandpa was Catholic, and he once told me, "I would cry when they didn't send me to church." He was even an altar boy at one point, a shocking fact for those who knew him in his later years. As an adult, he was a substance abuser prone to violence when under the influence and a deadbeat father to so many children that he couldn't even name them all. He wasn't exactly the poster boy for the Catholic Church. Nonetheless, when it was time to determine the type of ceremony for the funeral, I insisted on a traditional Catholic Mass; he would have wanted that.

Very few people attended the funeral. I was present, along with my dad, brother, Aunty Claire, and Camille, a childhood friend of my dad's. Two aunts that I had not previously met and their mother were also present. They were shocked when we contacted them about the funeral. They had assumed that Grandpa had died years ago. Rounding out the numbers in attendance was a small band of about four to six musicians and, of course, the priest.

I grew up with such little knowledge of the Catholic Church that I sat lost during the rites spoken at my grandfather's funeral. With the exception of the sermon, I had barely a clue as to what was transpiring. To show how truly ignorant I was, I assumed the band would be singing some type of Gregorian-like chant in Latin. When instead they performed a nice "modern" song in English, I thought, "Ah, yes. Vatican II."

I knew none of the responses to any of the sections of the Mass. And I wasn't the only one. Thank God for the band, because had they not been present, the priest would have had to respond to himself. Much of the funeral is now a blur, but I was true to my word—Grandpa had received a traditional Catholic farewell.

* * *

I have vague memories of the church in Brooklyn where I was dedicated. They are flashes that come and go. Women wearing dresses with matching head wraps of various colors—blue and white, maybe some others; I'm not sure. But I always sensed something there that felt ancestral, African. Years later, my mother confirmed my suspicions that some of the women there had ties to the African-influenced Spiritual Baptist faith, though the church itself was London Baptist.

My spiritual inheritance is a rich one, if only in theory. It is a confluence of religious and spiritual practices from disparate parts of the globe. My mother grew up Methodist but attended Anglican schools while growing up in Trinidad. Both of her parents were Methodist, but my grandmother should have been raised Catholic since in those days children were brought up with the religion of their father. However, since Papa apparently wasn't one for too much religion, he let his three daughters be raised under the religion of their mother, Mercy.

My father, on the other hand, didn't get too much religious training as a youth. He was what one might call a "non-practicing Catholic." His mother, Grandma Helen, grew up Catholic, though I'm not sure how often she went to church. And as we've seen, my paternal grandfather was such a devout Catholic that he apparently never wanted to miss Mass.

Cue: "Karele, Karele O (Oshun Karele)," "Ogun Ye Ku De Ye Baba," Ella Andall; "Shango," Roaring Lion

I imagine if one were to go further back in my lineage, one would most likely find evidence of indigenous and traditional African sacred practices. However, the traditions of my indigenous ancestors are not apparent to me; they seem to have been completely lost to time, or rather to the physical and epistemic violence wrought upon them by colonialism. In contrast, African sacred practices were retained to some degree in Trinidad. Even if some of those traditions were not maintained within my family—on my mother's side, we are rumored to have Yoruba and Ashanti roots—they were not completely eradicated and have managed to reemerge in various cultural art forms consumed by Trinidadians. Nonetheless, many of the "neo-traditional" African religions that developed in Trinidad have suffered the damaging effects of colonialism that rendered these traditions as "backward" or "evil" in the eyes of many people, including African-descended Trinidadians.

Neo-African religious traditions in Trinidad were marginalized for much of the twentieth century. The two most well-known practices belong to the Orisha and Spiritual (or

Shouter) Baptist faiths,[1] both of which were previously banned in Trinidad, forcing practitioners underground.[2] Times have changed, and both religions have come a long way since the days when my parents were growing up in Trinidad, when the practices of these groups were perceived as strange and weird, even demonic. Similar to the portrayal of Vodou in the media, these religious practices have been conflated with obeah, or "black magic."

Orisha practitioners in Trinidad were also ostracized for practicing a "polytheistic" religion. The orishas that are central to the religion have commonly been referred to as "gods," a misnomer that belies the fact that the religion is monotheistic. The orishas are better described as deities, or divine entities that are emissaries of a Supreme Being.[3] Trinidad Orisha and neo-traditional African sacred traditions found elsewhere in the Americas, such as Santería, Vodou, and Candomblé, were able to survive in predominantly Catholic states like Cuba, Haiti, and Brazil, respectively, in part because there is a similar cosmology at work in Catholicism and in these African-based traditions. Both consist of a Supreme God who is assisted by a host of lesser divinities—orishas, lwas, Catholic saints—who are physically closer to God and thus serve as intercessors on behalf of human beings.[4]

---

[1] Throughout the 20th century, the Orisha faith in Trinidad was commonly referred to as "Shango" or "Shango Baptist;" Spiritual Baptists were also known as "Shouter Baptists." The general public still sometimes uses these terms today.

[2] The Shouter Prohibition Ordinance outlawed the Spiritual Baptist faith in Trinidad from 1917-1951.

[3] Defining the orishas can be a tricky task. I know orisha practitioners who have used the term "gods" to describe the orishas. However, in English, the use of the term "gods" would imply that one is practicing polytheism. It's important to point out the limitations of language in this regard, as well as the importance of connotation when choosing language to describe certain phenomena.

[4] Because of the similarities between these seemingly different religious traditions, enslaved Africans were able to practice their respective religions under the guise of Catholicism.

Nonetheless, I remember learning about "world religions" in school and how traditional African sacred traditions, as well as other religions like Hinduism, were polytheistic religions, unlike the monotheistic religions of Judaism, Christianity, and Islam. As I got older and conducted my own studies, I came to understand that what I was taught was not entirely true. Through a self-study of Hinduism, I learned that the religion is monotheistic, with the various "gods" representing different manifestations of one Supreme Being.[5] It is not unlike the concept of the Holy Trinity—"God in three persons."[6] A couple of years ago, while talking with a graduate student from India who was also Hindu, I explained how I had only recently come to the realization that the religion is monotheistic. I asked him what he thought about the varying portrayals of Hinduism as monotheistic and polytheistic. He shrugged his shoulders and responded, "It doesn't matter. Whatever brings the person closer to God."

It is an interesting position and one that suggests that if there is only one God, then how God is conceptualized doesn't matter. We all worship the same Being, and if an intellectual debate on what to call a religious practice—i.e. monotheistic or polytheistic—deters one from God, then it is without merit.

If only we could all be so wise.

* * *

My religious upbringing was quite unlike that of my parents, grandparents, and ancestors. I grew up Pentecostal, attending a church in the East New York section of Brooklyn that had been started by several preachers from Jamaica. In the early years of the church, the membership consisted of

---

[5] Some also think of the orishas in similar terms.

[6] A line from the hymn "Holy, Holy, Holy" states, "God in three persons, blessed Trinity." Reginald Heber, "Holy, Holy, Holy," *Great Hymns of the Faith*-Blue, comp. John W. Peterson (Nashville: Brentwood Benson, 1993), 70. Interestingly, in the public sphere, Christianity is rarely discussed as being polytheistic although there is a similar process at work. However, in Christian scholarship, debates about Trinitarian monotheism (in contrast to its Unitarian equivalent) are not infrequent.

people from not only Jamaica, but also various Caribbean islands, including Trinidad, Barbados, and Grenada. But by and large, the congregation was Jamaican.

The Pentecostal Church

Fire, fire, fire
Fire fall on me
On the day of Pentecost
Fire fall on me
—"Fire, Fire, Fire," Pentecostal Chorus

Cue: "Caribbean Medley," Donnie McClurkin

Fiery is perhaps an apt description for the Pentecostal Church, a protestant denomination whose name refers to the mass baptism of people in the Holy Spirit that took place on the first Pentecost[7] following the crucifixion and resurrection of Christ. On this day, considered the beginning of the Christian church, the apostles and other believers had been gathered together in one place, when:

> Suddenly, there was a sound from heaven like the roaring of a mighty windstorm and it filled the house where they were sitting. Then, what looked like flames or tongues of fire appeared and settled on each of them. And everyone present was filled with the Holy Spirit and began speaking in other languages, as the Holy Spirit gave them this ability. At that time there were devout Jews from every nation living in Jerusalem. When they heard the loud noise, everyone came running, and they were bewildered to hear their own languages being spoken by believers.[8]

[7] Pentecost is a Jewish harvest festival.

[8] Acts 2: 1-6 (New Living Translation).

A similar occurrence was said to have taken place in 1906 during a revival at the Apostolic Faith Mission on Azusa Street in Los Angeles, CA. Those in attendance were said to have been filled with the Holy Spirit in a manner not unlike that mentioned in the Bible on the aforementioned day of Pentecost. Led by William J. Seymour, the son of former slaves, this revival is considered the event most significant to the birth of the Pentecostal movement.

The Pentecostal faith is both evangelical and charismatic. Practitioners believe in being "born again" (i.e. accepting Jesus Christ as their Lord and personal Savior), water baptism, and baptism in the Holy Spirit, as evidenced by the practice of speaking in tongues (glossolalia or xenoglossy). Pentecostals also believe in spreading the gospel, so that all may have the opportunity to enter the Kingdom of God.

Goodbye World

Goodbye world, I stay no longer with you
Goodbye pleasures of sin, I stay no longer with you
I've made up my mind to go God's way the rest of my life
I've made up my mind to go God's way the rest of my life
—"Goodbye World," Pentecostal Chorus

Pentecostals are supposed to adhere to a strict moral code, and once my father became entrenched in the religion, I was no longer allowed to wear pants and jewelry, and was supposed to "be in the world but not of it." The gold studs that can be seen adorning my ears in old photos were probably the last pair of earrings I owned until I bought a pair to wear at my high school prom.

I didn't much agree with many of the beliefs of the church. In some ways, I take after my Aunty Ruby who, unlike my grandmother, is not very religious. Instead, she adheres to many of the principles of metaphysics. And like me, she can be very critical of religion, not due to any disbelief in God, but because of the fallible nature of man who professes to know and teach God's word.

Aunty Ruby has said she doesn't understand "why America have so much church." I don't think I ever noticed until she brought it to my attention. But it is a fact that one can find throughout many of the predominantly black neighborhoods in Brooklyn several churches on one block, sometimes situated side-by-side. "God is Love," she would say. So, why then are people worshipping next to each other and not with each other?

Aunty Ruby was always asking deep philosophical questions about the nature of religion, God, and human beings. And like my great-aunt, my mind has always been inquisitive. Fortunately, despite my strict religious upbringing, critical thinking was always encouraged in our home. There were frequent discussions (which may have sounded like arguments to others) on the nature of religion and spirituality. Discussions of fate and predestination were especially common at the kitchen table or during long road trips. And the more I learned, the more questions I had, many of which have never been adequately answered in church.

Did I already say that I didn't like church very much growing up? Church was long—very long. Sunday school began at 9:45 a.m., and the main service began at 11:00 a.m. However, we sometimes did not get out of church until 3:00 p.m., because church ended at the direction of the Holy Spirit.

On Sunday mornings, my brother and I would get up early and leave with my dad to pick up other church members. In the earlier years, we'd travel to church in the station wagon that my dad had gotten from the pastor of the congregation—Pastor Bailey. Later, Dad used to drive the church van, picking up members and guests who lived in different sections of Brooklyn. We would travel north from East Flatbush to Crown Heights and then east through Brownsville and East New York, where our church was located. Once, I was running behind schedule. I walked out of the house and was heading towards the car parked across the street where my dad and brother had been waiting. As I neared the car, my father drove off without me. There's something quite insulting about a person driving off without you in the car, especially when you are approaching the door. I was fuming, and then I remembered, "You don't like church, remember?" I smiled and went about my business.

Sunday School

Most Sundays, I was successful in getting a ride to church. When we arrived, we would walk into the sanctuary and place our coats on the hangers that hung from three or four rolling coat stands at the back of the building. Then we'd make our way towards the front of the church for the opening of Sunday School.

I don't remember exactly how we started service, but I do remember coming together as a collective body to sing a few songs before splitting into our respective age groups. We used to sing songs like "Deep and Wide," "Round the Walls of Jericho," and "I'm in the Lord's Army," each one accompanied by a series of movements geared to encourage the participation of children.

It was there that I learned the order of all the books in the Bible through two songs, one for the Old Testament and one for the New Testament. I was most proud of my ability to sing the books of the twelve Minor Prophets in the Old Testament—Hosea, Joel, Amos, Obadiah, Jonah, Micah, Nahum, Habakkuk, Zephaniah, Haggai, Zachariah, Malachi. Their names were enough to send a child's tongue in knots. To this day, I sing these songs whenever I need to search for a Bible verse.

Hanging from one of the support beams to the left of the altar was a flip chart containing our weekly lessons. Each chart depicted a scene from the Bible, under which was the title of the morning lesson, as well as the "golden text," the main scripture reading for the lesson. Every Sunday morning, like robots, we would recite lines like following:

"The subject of this morning's lesson is 'God's Love.'"

"The golden text is taken from John chapter 3, verse 16. For God so loved the world that he gave his only begotten Son, that whosoever believeth in him should not perish, but have everlasting life."

Each week there was a new golden text with a new lesson to be learned. Our instructor would teach the lesson pertaining to the morning's topic before we closed Sunday school with a song and prayer. Although I wasn't particularly interested in Sunday school, I always had my golden text memorized, and I did learn a lot about the Bible that would serve me well in my future academic studies.

After Sunday school, we would head to the kitchen at the back of the church to be treated to snacks consisting of cookies or wafers and Kool-Aid. I'm not sure feeding children sugar before the start of a long service was a wise idea, but then again, whatever outbursts there were most often came from the adults.

Sunday Worship

The service would begin soon after we partook of our mid-morning meal. Congregants gathered in the main sanctuary and took their seats. Every Sunday, I sat in the second pew, flanked by my brother on my left and Sister Bailey, the pastor's wife, to my right. Once most people had been seated, the song leader, standing at the podium in the center of the pulpit, would begin to lead the congregation in a devotional song. With hands raised and bodies gently swaying, the church would sing.

Heavenly Father, we appreciate you
Heavenly Father, we appreciate you

We love you, adore you, we bow done before you
Heavenly Father, we appreciate you[9]

There were a number of devotional songs from which to choose; I didn't much care for them. For the most part, I thought they were depressing, with a penchant for inducing weeping and other emotional states from congregants. The songs were sung with such emotion that one could sense (or at least I could) the agony that certain church members were feeling that particular morning. Needless to say, I was happy at the conclusion of the opening song, when the song leader would ask a member of the church to officially open the service with prayer.

"Heavenly Father, we just want to thank you for waking us up this morning and allowing us to come into your house. We thank you for your goodness."

"Yes, Lord," one congregant interjects.

"We thank you for your manifold blessings upon us."

"Hallelujah!" shouts a sister sitting towards the back of the church. "Thank you, Father."

"We pray that you will bless the song leader. Open up her voice so that she may guide us in giving YOU the praise, the honor, and the glory. Touch the musicians. Touch the preacher, dear Father, so that he might bring us your Word."

"Yes, Father," says a voice to my left.

"Bless those who are still on their way, and bring them here safely. All these things we pray in Jesus name. Amen."

"Amen," the congregation responds.

"Glory to God," says the song leader.

No one responds.

"I don't think you heard me. I said, 'Glory to God!'"

"Praise Him!"

"Hallelujah!"

"Let us begin the service in the attitude of praise. Please turn your hymnals to hymn number thirteen."

---

[9] "Heavenly Father, We Appreciate You," Pentecostal Chorus.

Praise ye the Lord, the Almighty, the King of Creation!
O my soul, praise Him, for He is thy health and salvation!
All ye who hear, Now to His temple draw near;
Join me in glad adoration.[10]

In the early years of the church, we had musicians who would play an introduction before the congregation would join in singing. However, in subsequent years the church population would dwindle as many of the older members retired and either returned to their respective homelands or moved south to Florida. Most of our church musicians followed suit, and in their absence the song leader would simply begin singing.

For each song, we'd sing every verse and chorus (or refrain). At times, after singing all of the verses, the song leader might signal the congregation to repeat a particular verse before returning to the chorus and ending the song. This way, songs could be stretched out for longer periods of time.

We used two hymnals, *Great Hymns of the Faith* and *Heavenly Highway Hymns.*[11] The latter we only used on Second Sundays, which I appreciated since it was my least favorite of the two. The songs in both hymns represent a body of work that is familiar to people across several Protestant denominations. Popular songs, like "I Surrender All" and "Blessed Assurance," as well as Christmas hymns, such as "Joy to the World" and "Hark! The Herald Angels Sing," can be found in both hymnals. Because of my familiarity with the songs in these collections, it was easy to visit several non-Pentecostal churches and be able to participate in their worship services. However, although the songs may have been the same, the practice of worship was not necessarily transferable.

It was through the hymnal that I also developed some

---

[10] Joachim Neander, "Praise Ye the Lord, the Almighty," *Great Hymns of the Faith*-Blue, comp. John W. Peterson (Nashville: Brentwood Benson, 1993), 13.

[11] John W. Peterson, comp., *Great Hymns of the Faith*-Blue (Nashville: Bentwood Benson, 1993) and Luther G. Presley, comp., *Heavenly Highway Hymns* (Dallas: Stamps-Baxter, 1956).

rudimentary music literacy. I became fascinated with musical notes and how they changed with the rise and fall of each pitch. The *Heavenly Highway Hymns* that we used had funny looking notes that were shaped as ovals, squares, and triangles. It would be years before I realized that these "shape notes" were more than just decoration, and that the shapes of the notes actually represented a specific pitch. These notes were designed to aid in "sight-singing," the practice of singing a melody by looking at the notes on the page. I don't know if anyone in the church was able to sight-sing, or more specifically, understood how to utilize shape notes. Most of us learned the hymns and various church choruses orally and by rote.

Prayer and Consecration

Is any among you afflicted? let him pray. Is any merry? let him sing psalms.

Is any sick among you? let him call for the elders of the church; and let them pray over him, anointing him with oil in the name of the Lord:

And the prayer of faith shall save the sick, and the Lord shall raise him up; and if he have committed sins, they shall be forgiven him.

Confess your faults one to another, and pray one for another, that ye may be healed. The effectual fervent prayer of a righteous man availeth much.

—James 5:13-16, King James Version

Cue: "The Prayers," J. Moss; "Faith," Kirk Franklin's Nu Nation

Once while in high school, my roommate and I decided to say prayers together. I'm not sure what promoted the occasion, or if we ever said prayers together afterwards, but at some point it was my turn to beseech the Lord.

"Lord, I pray that you will protect us from ghosts, goblins, aliens, the Devil himself, imps…"

And so I continued, with a laundry list of supernatural, evil entities, praying that God would protect my roommate and me from every manner of evil in the world; I tried to name them all, too. My roommate laughed. I didn't care. The way I saw it, better to be safe than sorry. This world ain't easy, you know.

The first prayer that I was taught was very much unlike the one I'd given that night as a sophomore in high school; it was the Lord's Prayer. David and I were taught to say that prayer every night before going to bed. Prayer is considered an integral part of the Pentecostal faith. It is through prayer that one communicates with God, and it is through faith that one's prayers are answered.

Although we pray at several points throughout a typical Sunday church service, there is a special point in the service that is dedicated specifically to "prayer and consecration." After singing several songs, the song leader would prepare the church for this section by choosing a song that generally brings comfort to the listener by extolling God's love and kindness towards His sheep. A song like "Blessed Assurance" or "Come, Ye Disconsolate" would be appropriate.

"We are going to sing Hymn #286 for prayer and consecration. That's Hymn #286. If you have a need today, brethren, come to the altar knowing that God answers prayers. Amen?"

"Amen!"

Come, ye disconsolate, where'er ye languish—
Come to the mercy seat, fervently kneel
Here bring your wounded hearts,
Here tell your anguish;
Earth has no sorrow that heav'n cannot heal.[12]

---

[12] Thomas Moore and Thomas Hastings, "Come, Ye Disconsolate." *Great Hymns of the Faith*-Blue, comp. John W. Peterson (Nashville: Brentwood Benson, 1993), 286.

After singing through the last verse, the congregation would continue singing, repeating specified verses or just the chorus (depending on the song), as people filed down the aisles towards the altar. Then one or several of the church deacons or reverends would begin anointing with oil the heads of those who had come seeking answers to prayer.

As a child, I very rarely went to the prayer line. It's not that I never had a need, but I've always had a "sensitive spirit," and I didn't want to catch any bad vibes from people laying hands on me. Yes, I was in church, but my spirit knew better than to trust everyone who claimed to be God-fearing.

Eventually, one of the church ministers would begin preaching.

"The Bible says that 'men ought always to pray and not to'?"

"Faint," the congregation responds.[13]

"So we come to the throne of God in faith, believing that He will fill whatever needs we have. Do you believe that God answers prayers?"

Members of the congregation respond with shouts of "Yes!" and "Amen!"

"As the song writer says, 'Let Jesus fix it for you,'" the preacher continues. "'He knows just what to do. Whenever you pray, let the Lord have His?"

"Way!" the congregation shouts.

"And so, believers, let Jesus fix it for you. Bow your heads. Heavenly Father, we come before your throne of grace asking that you touch Sister Headley."

As he speaks, the minister's words are punctuated with interjections from members of the congregation. An "Amen!" here, and a "Hallelujah!" there can be heard throughout his prayer.

"Lord, only you know her condition. We pray that you will put your hand upon her."

"Yes, Father."

---

[13] Luke 18: 1 (King James Version).

"Lord, we pray that you will deliver her from the hands of the enemy; bind every work of the devil. We pray that you will bless everyone who comes before you today seeking favor, and that everyone will leave this place knowing that you have delivered us, for no weapon formed against us shall prosper!"

"Glory!"

"We are more than conquerors through the blood of Jesus Christ. Have your way, Lord, and we pray that you will cause your face to shine upon us. In Jesus name we pray. Amen and Amen. Hallelujah! Go back to your seats with the knowledge and assurance that you are healed. Our God is a miracle worker. Don't you know our God is a miracle worker? There is wonder working power in the blood! Amen! Don't you know how He healed the sick? How He made the lame to walk and the dumb to talk. You see, everywhere He went, my Lord was doing good! Amen! Let's sing that chorus as you return to your seats."

And so the church would launch into song.

Everywhere He went
He was doing good
He taught the Beatitudes
He fed the multitudes
Everywhere He went

When the people saw Him
The lame walking
The dumb talking as they should
Everywhere He went
My Lord was doing good[14]

After prayer and consecration, the song leader would lead the congregation in singing several popular choruses, moving from one song seamlessly into the next, in essence, creating a medley.

---

[14] "Everywhere He Went," Pentecostal Chorus.

However, our segue to our seats after prayer and consecration didn't always run smoothly. Sometimes, as people were walking back to their seats, someone would be overcome with the Spirit and begin to shout.

"Hallelujah! Hallelujah! Thank you, Jesus!"

During these outpourings, I would sit and watch people jump up and down or simply fall out on the floor, their bodies quivering as they cried to the Lord. All the grief and pain they felt was plain for everyone to see. Literally, they placed their all—their very selves—on the altar of sacrifice. Church mothers would inevitably come to assist, helping the afflicted off the floor and walking them back to their seats. There were times when people were simply left at the altar until they felt good and ready to leave; church service just continued around them.

As a child, I don't think I really got it—what *that* was. It didn't scare me; at a certain point, it had simply become normal to me. But as an adult, I came to realize just how much we humans embody the pain and hardships of life. At some point, the poison in one's cup runneth over and needs to be released. And if it doesn't come out, it stays in and one implodes, self-destructs. We become infected with disease and our bodies break down, or we inject all manner of toxic substances into our bodies to kill the thing we cannot eradicate and end up still killing ourselves. No, better to leave it there at the altar. As the songwriter says, "Take your burdens to the Lord and leave it there."[15]

Eventually we would move on to other aspects of the service, such as the reading of the Holy Scripture. The entire congregation and the person leading this segment of the service would read a passage of scripture specifically selected for the morning's service. Sometimes this scripture was read in unison. However, most often it was read in an "alternate manner"—the person leading would read one verse, followed by the congregation reading the next. The last verse was always read in unison.

---

[15] Charles A. Tindley, "Leave It There," *Great Hymns of Faith*-Blue, comp. John W. Peterson (Nashville: Brentwood Benson, 1993), 353.

The collection of tithes and offering was another staple of our Sunday service.

"At this time, we are going to sing 'O, Magnify the Lord' as we lift our morning tithes and offering."

The ushers would come to the front of the church and stand with their collection plates while the congregation sung the specified chorus, simultaneously digging in their pocketbooks and coat pockets for their offerings to the Lord. Then they would get up, march down the closest aisle, and deliver their dollars, checks, and coins. Once the last straggler had moseyed up the aisle, the song leader would ask one of the ushers to "bless the morning tithes and offering." There was never any awkward solicitation of monies prior to the collection of tithes and offering. No reading from scriptures regarding the importance of giving unto the Lord and shaming people into giving money. When I would visit churches that conducted their services in that way, it always made me feel a little uneasy. I liked that my little church did not try to guilt people into giving tithes and offering, and I always loved when Brother Farr, one of the ushers, would simply say:

"Bless those who had, and those who had not, to give. In Jesus name we pray. Amen."

When I think about the goodness of Jesus
And all that He's done for me
My soul cries out, Hallelujah!
Thank God for saving me
—"When I Think About the Goodness of Jesus,"
Pentecostal Chorus

"Scripture showers" and the "testimony shout" were aspects of service that did not occur every Sunday, but only on occasion and usually after the collection of tithes and offering. During scripture showers, those in attendance—both young and old— would pop out of their seats and recite a word of scripture. It almost felt like we were playing a game in church, one in which mainly the adults participated. And from what I can remember, they were the only ones who participated in the "testimony shout," although I don't believe children were prevented from doing so. During this section of the service, congregants were encouraged to stand up and give a "testimony" regarding what the Lord had done for them. You never knew how long a testimony was going to last. Some were short and sweet, and others had you watching the minutes go by. Oh, how West Indians love to explatiate.[16]

The African Legacy

During times like this, I might listen to the testimony, or sometimes I'd zone out and my eyes would wander, looking at the various images that adorned the church. On many occasions my eyes would fixate on a depiction of the crucifixion that was embedded in a piece of tapestry that hung at the back of the church, just to the right of the pulpit. It was a familiar scene: Jesus nailed to a cross and flanked on both sides by two criminals who were also condemned to die. A Roman soldier pierces his side with a spear. The rendering, like so many others, depicted Jesus with European features. While the Jesus that confronted us on a weekly basis through pictures and paintings was unmistakably white, with dirty blond hair and bluish eyes, the atmosphere in the church seemed far removed from a European ethos.

Africa's legacy was always felt strongly in our church. I'm not sure if other people thought much about it, but I did. The music especially echoed the calls of our ancestors, to which we responded. There were several characteristics of music from West and Central Africa that were certainly present during Sunday services and other church functions. There was

[16] In Trinidadian parlance, explatiate refers to the ability of speakers to both explain and expound (or expatiate) on a given topic, sometimes with the only purpose of hearing themselves talk.

communal participation and call and response. Polyrhythms abounded, and people moved and danced to the music.

While we had musicians who played the piano, organ, guitar, and bass, the function of our church musicians was not to provide the music so much as to guide the music. We were all tasked with making a "joyful noise" unto the Lord. Some congregants played tambourines, both with and without drumheads. Sister Lawrence played a marac (always one, never two). Others clapped on a variety of beats—some clapped on the 1 and 3, others on the 2 and 4. And there were those who clapped on the offbeats, providing some rhythmic variation and musical excitement. People varied their claps as they saw fit, as the Spirit moved them.

Africa was present, but largely via the Caribbean. The singing of church songs, both the hymns and choruses, but especially the choruses, signified a Caribbean ethos. The words alone, pronounced by Caribbean voices with Caribbean accents, created a space mostly unknown to those who were not already a part of it. And because of the strong Jamaican presence in the church, the music perhaps most reflected that island's musical heritage. Most of the choruses consisted of a simple I-IV-V progression, but the piano and guitar comps, as well as the bass lines, had a kind of rock steady or reggae groove.

Dance and movement were other legacies of Africa and the Caribbean brought into the church. The Spirit working through the music encouraged people to embody the rhythms and the words they heard. They swayed their bodies; they danced. And when I say they danced, they *danced*. Not everybody, but there were those who were known for their fancy footwork. We used to joke that we know all who used to find themselves in the clubs back "home."

Sister Lewin was one of the great ones. Her face fades from memory, but her spirit does not. She would emerge from the pews when the Spirit caught her and waltz down the aisles to the front of the church. She'd do a few steps forward and then take a few steps backwards. Though I loved to watch her dance, there was always a fear that I might become a victim of her spiritual frenzy. Catching the spirit was contagious, or so I thought. Whenever one of those church mothers was touched by the Holy Ghost, I was afraid I would come down with the same affliction, particularly since they had a penchant for grabbing other church members to join them in their holy dance.

Back to Service

Cue: "My God, My God, My God," "Completely Yes," Sandra Crouch; "Take Me Back," "Soon and Very Soon," Andraé Crouch

For many people, the main event during the Sunday morning service was the sermon, but for me, I wanted to hear the choir sing. We had a nice-sized choir during the early years of the church, before members started moving south to Florida in the 1990s, when two sister churches were founded. The choir was good, too. We had several talented voices, including that of Denise, the church organist and choir director, who eventually became my first real piano teacher.

Our church choir didn't sing traditional hymns or choruses, at least not often. Most of the songs they sang were songs that had been or were currently popular on the gospel charts. While reminiscing on this time period, I realized that many of the songs that I recalled the choir singing were by either Andraé Crouch or his twin sister, Sandra Crouch, reflecting their dominance (especially Andraé's) in the gospel world during my early youth.

When the church membership was larger, the choir would sing twice on Sundays, once at the beginning of church—after the opening prayer but before the singing of the hymns—and then again before the sermon.

The Sermon

Pastor Bailey stood looking out at the congregation from the pulpit and said, "December 5, '41." I immediately knew where this was heading.

Sometimes I think I know the date that Pastor Bailey became saved better than my own birthday. It was a date that he would often repeat during his lengthy sermons, which often began between half past eleven and noon. And then the hours seemed to just go by. David sat to my left with his head down and eyes closed. I'm not sure how he appeared to others. Perhaps he looked like he was meditating. I assure you he was not. He was sleeping, and he did that a lot. I can't say that I blame him. It was a lot to sit through those sermons. I mean, some of the stories Pastor Bailey told were interesting, and we remember them fondly to this day. But sometimes, and especially as a kid, you just wanted to go home.

I would feel a certain excitement when it was clear that service was winding down. After the sermon, the minister who preached would often lead (or ask someone to lead) the church in a song that had some relevance to the morning's message. Afterwards, a prayer thanking the Lord for his word and for continued blessings would close the service. And I was free.

The Lord's Supper

King of my life, I crown Thee now –
Thine shall the glory be;
Lest I forget Thy thorn-crowned brow,
Lead me to Calvary
—"Lead Me to Calvary," Jennie Evelyn Hussey[17]

[17] Jennie Evelyn Hussey, "Lead Me to Calvary," *Great Hymns of the Faith-*Blue, comp. John W. Peterson (Nashville: Bentwood Benson, 1993), 124.

Every first Sunday, at the conclusion of the regular service, the church would busy itself in preparation for communion. Instead of the standard meet-and-greet at church's end, those in attendance would shuffle their seats so that all those who were saved and baptized in the Holy Spirit, and thus eligible to take communion, could sit in the center pews, while those who could not (or would not) partake in communion sat off to the side.

On those Sundays, David and I would leave our seats next to Sister Bailey in the second pew and move off to the side where the choir traditionally sat. I never really liked this rearrangement, as I felt that I, along with several others, was ostracized from the rest of the congregation. Nonetheless, I still participated in this portion of the service, turning my hymnal to the specified page and singing songs, with the baptized and non-baptized alike, on the suffering and death of Christ.[18]

Before communion was taken, the minister leading this portion of the service would read a section of scripture, written by the Apostle Paul, that details the importance of the ceremonial reenactment of the Lord's Supper.

> For I have received of the Lord that which also I delivered unto you, That the Lord Jesus the *same* night in which he was betrayed took bread:
>
> And when he had given thanks, he brake *it*, and said, 'Take, eat: this is my body, which is broken for you: this do in remembrance of me.'
>
> After the same manner also *he took* the cup, when he had supped, saying, 'This cup is the new testament in my blood: this do ye, as oft as ye drink *it*, in remembrance of me. For as often as ye eat this bread, and drink this cup, ye do shew the Lord's death till he

[18] The songs most commonly sung during communion were "When I Survey the Wondrous Cross," "Why," "Lead Me to Calvary," "Jesus Paid It All," and "At the Cross."

> come. Wherefore whosoever shall eat this bread, and drink *this* cup of the Lord, unworthily, shall be guilty of the body and blood of the Lord.
>
> But let a man examine himself, and so let him eat of *that* bread, and drink of *that* cup. For he that eateth and drinketh unworthily, eateth and drinketh damnation to himself, not discerning the Lord's body. For this cause many *are* weak and sickly among you, and many sleep. For if we would judge ourselves, we should not be judged.
>
> But when we are judged, we are chastened of the Lord, that we should not be condemned with the world. Wherefore, my brethren, when ye come together to eat, tarry one for another. And if any man hunger, let him eat at home; that ye come not together unto condemnation. And the rest will I set in order when I come.[19]

After reading the scripture, a prayer was said, and then wafers representing the body of Christ were passed out as the congregation sang one of the hymns traditionally sung for the Lord's Supper. Once all of the wafers were passed out, the minister would say a short blessing before all those permitted to take communion would collectively and symbolically partake in the Lord's body. Some people took their time, chewing every morsel, while others consumed their portion quickly.

A similar process took place for the drinking of the wine (grape juice, in our church) that represented the blood of Christ. A prayer was said before the "wine," already poured into small communion glasses, was passed out to the accompaniment of music. Then, after a short blessing, the "wine" was consumed.

[19] I Corinthians 11:23-34 (King James Version).

As a young child, communion had a way of getting my salivary glands worked up, especially after several hours in church without eating much. I often wondered how the "bread" tasted, and I already knew that the "cup" was filled with grape juice. And I liked grape juice. On one particular first Sunday, after communion had been given and church had ended, Pastor Bailey squelched my curiosity. Now, I don't remember if I asked or he offered, but he dipped his hand into the communion plate and brought forth a piece of "bread" and gave it to me. I finally had in my hands the object of my desire for several years, and like all things lusted after, it was thoroughly disappointing. No flavor.

Blessed Holy Ghost Come Down

Being filled with the Holy Ghost is an important part of the Pentecostal faith, but I never wanted the Holy Ghost to come down on me. I even prayed as much. I never liked dealing with spirits, even good ones. When it finally did, I never wanted to let go.

Despite my father being a preacher, I went a long time before I was baptized. I had tried at least once in high school, and maybe again in college. When I approached my high school's chaplain about getting baptized, he began asking me a lot of questions.

"Why do you want to get baptized?"

I hardly remember the questions that followed, but the first question was enough for me to give up on the enterprise. It has always been my belief that my faith is no one's business except mine and my God's. God and I have always been cool, and public declarations of fidelity based on other people's terms have always bothered me. When I finally did get baptized, it wasn't because any mere mortal had told me to do so—God did. I knew that it was divinely ordained, because although I had made up my mind to answer whatever questions church officials had concerning my desire to be baptized, no one in the church asked me a single question regarding the matter.

I was simply required to attend a short class a few minutes before the baptism.

The church where I'd eventually be baptized was evangelical and so had some similarities to the church in which I'd grown up. However, most of the congregation was white; nonetheless, there was a decent number of people of color. The music-making was largely a function of the church choir, although song lyrics were displayed on several large screens posted around the church. Those who wanted to join in the singing were not discouraged. By and large, I attended the service to hear the sermon. I wasn't particularly moved by the music, although there was one singer, an African American woman, who always sang in a way that I found touching. She was one of several lead singers, so she didn't always perform during Sunday services. However, the night of my baptism she did.

Cue: "Break Every Chain," Tasha Cobbs

There was a huge storm the night I got baptized. When I left home, the roads were fairly clear, but about halfway through the trip snow began falling at a steady and rapid pace. By the time I arrived at the church, there was a significant amount of snow on the ground.

For a while, it seemed like I was going to be the only one baptized that day. No one else had arrived, presumably deterred by the ensuing storm. One of the ministers, Reverend Mike, even began talking about how special I was to be the only one baptized that day, until two more candidates walked in, much to the minister's chagrin. He was almost finished with the baptismal class when they entered the room where we were gathered, and so Reverend Mike extended his talk before instructing the new candidates to change into their clothes for the ceremony. I was already dressed, so I waited for them to suit up. When they were done getting ready, we all proceeded to the main sanctuary for a few songs of praise and worship. Then the woman whose voice I loved began to sing a haunting version of Tasha Cobbs' rendition of "Break Every Chain."

There is power in the name of Jesus
There is power in the name of Jesus
There is power in the name of Jesus
To break every chain, break every chain, break every chain
To break every chain, break every chain, break every chain

The two other candidates and I arose from our seats and walked single-file towards the front of the sanctuary, where we walked through a door leading us to a room behind the pulpit. As the singing continued in the main sanctuary, we readied ourselves for the plunge.

If memory serves me correct, I was the first to be baptized. As I walked into the water, which was surprisingly and pleasantly warm, the announcer stated that I was from Brooklyn and saved twenty-four years. I walked to Reverend Mike and his wife Reverend Teresa, who were already in the water. They instructed me to put my hands over my chest, and asked me if I had accepted Jesus as my Lord and Savior. I said, "I have."

Reverend Teresa then said something, and I was dunked backwards into the water. Unfortunately, I neglected to hold my nose, which made for a rather uncomfortable experience, maybe even more so for those who were watching the ceremony unfold on the large screens in the main sanctuary.

I went home feeling unbelievably clean. I felt so clean that I didn't even take a shower, this despite being a moderate germaphobe. Then later that night I had the most amazing experience. The only way to describe it is as pure ecstasy. All my senses were alive; my body was tingling. I felt like I was floating in a cocoon of cosmic nothingness that was filled with everything good. I felt safe. I felt loved. I felt at peace.

When I woke up the following morning, I was no longer sure what I had experienced was real. Was it a dream? Regardless, I kept praying for the Holy Spirit to come down again. I wanted that feeling again. I tried for several days to return to that place, with no success.

I would later think to myself, and sometimes chuckle, about the similarities between seemingly disparate religions like Christianity and African sacred traditions. From the power of water in religious ceremonies to the notion of merging with the divine, there is a shared commonality, although we have a tendency to talk about them in very different ways.

Well, it turned out that the Holy Ghost was not such a bad thing after all, but there were other types of ghosts and spirits lurking, and they weren't all named Casper.

PART II: OF GHOSTS AND OBEAH

As I reach the street
A tall gentleman I meet
I was feeling so happy
To tell him my fright in de cemetery
He said, "I can understand
You're a wild young man,
But still you not to be blamed,
When I was alive I was just the same."
—"Love in the Cemetery," Lord Kitchener

Cue: "Love in the Cemetery," Lord Kitchener

We lived a few blocks from a big cemetery. On occasions, my brother or I would lose our bus pass. As a result, we would have to turn our four-bus commute to our middle school in Bushwick into a two-bus commute by walking about two thirds of a mile to catch our first bus. On those days, we would have to pass the dreaded Holy Cross Cemetery. Sometimes, as we passed this final resting place for the dead, there would be a dense fog that sat on the tombstones. My steps would quicken, and my once-cool walk would morph into a run that tried to masquerade itself as a typical, quick-paced, New York stride.

A little further up the road, we'd pass dead chickens strewn about the sidewalk. Walking in the other direction, towards the Newkirk Avenue subway, I'd sometimes see cracked eggs splashed on a street corner. For some reason, I was never too concerned about the dead chickens or the cracked eggs, despite knowing full well they likely were part of some kind of *simi dimi.*[20] I'd merely think to myself "Haitians" or "voodoo". But that cemetery gave me the chills. I was very much afraid of ghosts and, in my mind, Holy Cross Cemetery was full of them.

The belief in spirits and people who can access and manipulate the supernatural to do their bidding is commonplace in the Caribbean. In several parts of the Caribbean, such work is called *obeah*. The term generally has a bad connotation and is often considered to be synonymous with "black magic," "sorcery," and "witchcraft." However, the practice is much more complicated; obeah can be used for "good," as we'll later see in a case involving my grandfather.

Margarite Fernández Olmos and Lizabeth Paravisini-Gebert provide what I think is a comprehensive and useful description of the term as used in the Caribbean. They describe obeah as "a set of hybrid or creolized beliefs dependent on ritual invocation, fetishes, and charms" that "incorporates two very distinct categories of practice."

> The first involves "the casting of spells for various purposes, both good and evil: protecting oneself, property, family, or loved ones; harming real or perceived enemies; and bringing fortune in love, employment, personal or business pursuits" (Frye 1997: 198). The second incorporates traditional African-derived healing practices based on the application of considerable knowledge of herbal and animal medicinal properties. Obeah, thus conceived, is not a religion so much as a system of beliefs rooted in Creole notions of spirituality which acknowledges the existence and power of the supernatural world and incorporates into its prac-

---

[20] In this context, simi dimi refers to "black magic," or some kind of secretive dealing with the supernatural.

tices witchcraft, sorcery, magic, spells, and healing (Frye 1997: 198).[21]

Thus, as a set of practices, obeah can be used for both "good" and "evil." However, in general, the term has a negative connotation, even when used to assist people, as evident in a story my grandfather once told me.

Melda, oh you makin' wedding plans
Carrying meh name to obeah man
All you do, you can't get through
I still ent go marry to you
—"Obeah Wedding," Mighty Sparrow

Cue: "Obeah Wedding," Mighty Sparrow

My grandfather was a ladies' man. He was also not a very nice man. Sometimes, not nice things happen to not nice people.

One day, he told me a story of how he was poisoned but saved by obeah. He was working at the gas station by Four Roads in Diego Martin and was talking with a lady friend.

"We were just friends," he assures me.

Apparently, a woman he had been dating saw him talking to his "friend," and she promptly confronted him. She was upset, but my grandfather insisted there was nothing inappropriate going on.

On another day, the woman he had been dating went to the aforementioned gas station and brought him some food. He said the food was so good.

"It tasted sweeet!"

---

[21] Margarite Fernández Olmos and Lizabeth Paravisini-Gebert, *Creole Religions of the Caribbean: An Introduction from Vodou and Santería to Obeah and Espiritismo*, 2nd Edition (New York and London: New York University Press, 2011), 155.

Unfortunately, what sweet in the belly go sour in de bam bam, if you get my drift. Grandpa began to feel ill, so ill that the other mechanics told him to go lie down in a back room at the station. They eventually called my great-grandmother, Tantie Maggie, who came to retrieve him and take him to the hospital. But the doctors couldn't figure out what was wrong with him, and he was becoming extremely sick.

Hearing word of his illness, Tantie Maggie's sister, Petite, took Grandpa to an obeah man she had been dating. This obeah man told Grandpa that he had been poisoned—the bones of a dead person had been crushed and placed in his food. In order to get better, he would have to undergo a cleansing; it consisted of a bath that Grandpa remembered contained saffron (or was it turmeric?) because it turned his skin yellow. That bath saved his life. Nonetheless, Grandpa was upset that his aunt had taken him to an obeah man.

"But Grandpa, he saved your life!"

Traigo yerba santa pa' la garganta...
Traigo abrecamino pa' su destino...
Y con esa yerba se casa usted[22]
—"Yerbero moderno," Celia Cruz

Cue: "Yerbero moderno," Celia Cruz

Obeah men and women are known for the ability to heal people through their dealings with the spiritual world and knowledge of the medicinal properties of herbs. However, not everyone with knowledge of "bush medicine" is considered an obeah practitioner, though there may be some overlap in their knowledge and skill sets.

I sat talking with Aunty Ruby on her bed in Diego Martin,

[22] The song title translates as "modern herbalist." Celia Cruz sings: I bring "yerba santa" (holy herb) for your throat/I bring "abrecamino" (open path, or that which opens pathways) for your destiny/And with that herb, you'll get married.

when she reached over and picked up a receipt that was resting atop the small bookshelf next to the bed. Somebody had ordered a six-inch pizza and one ham and cheese sandwich from the Pizza Boys at Piarco International Airport. Aunty Ruby looked at the receipt and carefully turned it over to the back side, which was blank. Then, in a calligraphy known only to people of a certain age, she began to write. At the top of the page she wrote: “Herman Bedlow.” Then she proceeded to write the following:

Calabash—heart
Coreilli—clean the blood
Soursop—to sleep
Vervine—cooling

And at the very bottom she wrote, “Young leaves.”

Aunty Ruby had been suffering from a condition where she was sweating all the time, losing weight, and was constantly tired. The doctor had given her pills for her thyroid, but she seemed to be getting sicker. She traveled to Tobago for some reason unknown to me, or at least I don’t recall. While there, she complained about her symptoms to her cousin, Herman Bedlow, who encouraged her to stop taking “those pills.” He promptly gave her a prescription for some “bush tea,” which was to be made with the young leaves of five different plants. (Aunty Ruby only wrote down the names of four plants on the back of the Pizza Boys receipt; she couldn’t remember the fifth.) She promised Herman that she would make and drink the tea.

With prescription in hand, Aunty Ruby returned to Trinidad, and instead of immediately making the tea, she began to have doubts.

“Like he trying to kill me with this thing,” she told Aunty Elaine.

Aunty Elaine didn’t think so. She encouraged her sister to make and drink the tea, citing that she had promised her cousin that she would do so. So, somewhat reluctantly, Aunty Ruby prepared her bush tea. She drank it, and her symptoms went away. In effect, she was cured.

My interest in this particular part of Aunty Ruby's life was more than cursory. The day when Aunty Ruby began telling me about her illness and its symptoms, it was as though she was reading a page from my life. I had been afflicted with a thyroid-related illness at a young age, and most of my thyroid gland had been removed. The result was that I was left with a supposedly incurable disease that has wreaked much havoc on my mind and body over the ensuing decades. My experience of having an auto-immune illness at a young age, and subsequently interacting with several medical professionals over the years, has led me to have an extremely cautious view of Western medicine and the pharmaceutical industry. I have witnessed first-hand the ways in which doctors have been trained to excise body parts and/or mask symptoms with pills, rather than seek and treat the root causes of the illness. Many are trained to have more faith in synthetic, man-made drugs than in holistic remedies that include herbal medicines.

I wish Uncle Herman had been around before my thyroid was removed, not just so that he could have possibly cured my illness, but because he clearly had knowledge of how to use natural resources for healing; I would have loved to be his apprentice. Still, during my stays in Trinidad, I tried to learn as much as I could about the different local plants and their medicinal properties. I can't say I learned much, although my cousins' mom, Ann, did use *ditay payee*[23] to help ease an eye infection that I had.

* * *

Although knowledge of medicinal healing is one of the functions of an obeah man or woman, equally important is knowledge of preventative measures, or how to protect oneself from the harm that others would try to inflict. For example, it's been said that one should flush hair and nail clippings down

---

[23] An herb (Capraria biflora, Fam. Scrophulariacea). Renato Tomei, *Forbidden Fruits: The Secret Names of Plants in Caribbean Culture* (Perugia: Morlacchi Editore, 2008), 40.

the toilet, lest someone use them to "wuk obeah" on you. Protection is important because, as we saw with Grandpa, you never know who might be trying to do you harm. In Trinidad, there are many stories of well-known evil entities that prey on unsuspecting victims. I've been hearing such stories from my dad (and to a lesser extent my mom) since I was a child. Those stories can still give me chills today; they describe personal encounters with the beings and creatures that encompass the folktales of the island.

The Soucouyant

I was a child—still in single digits—when my dad told me about the soucouyant. The soucouyant is a person who through the use of obeah can transform from a physical being into a ball of fire and then travels under the cover of darkness into homes, sucking the blood of those inside.

My dad explained how a soucouyant used to suck Aunty Maggie's blood. She would wake up with the tell-tale blue marks on her skin. This upset me because I loved Tantie Maggie.

"If they knew who the soucouyant was, why didn't they get them?" I asked my dad incredulously.

"I don't know. They couldn't prove it, " my father responded to my inquiry.

I put up my fists in a fighting pose.

"If she [the soucouyant] comes by me, I'm going to get her," I said.

Yes, I was a real badjohn. My father continued with his story.

"One day when I was small and staying with my grandmother, the soucouyant visited."

"How did you know?" I asked.

"Well, my grandmother had put me to bed, and she had placed a white sheet over me as I slept. In the morning when she woke up, the sheet was stained red, and there was a blood trail from where I slept to the door."

"What?!" I shouted in disbelief. "What happened?!"

"Apparently, my blood didn't agree with the soucouyant, and it vomited up my blood, leaving a trail as it left the house."

Every time my dad tells that story, I say, "That's how we knew you were going to be a preacher." He had that crucifix, send-thee-back-to-hell kind of blood.[24]

My father had many other stories, like the time my great-grandfather, Pappy, encountered a *diablesse*,[25] a beautiful woman who ensnares men with her charms, and whose supernatural powers and diabolical intent are revealed only by the cloven hoof that substitutes for her foot. Then there was the time my father and his uncle, Ashton, were pursued by a "big dog."[26] This was no ordinary dog, my dad explained, but one whose size indicated that the supernatural was invoked through the use of obeah.

"What happened?"

"What do you mean, what happened? We ran!" my dad chuckled.

Well, Ashton ran, and my father went along for the ride. My great-uncle grabbed my father by the wrist and ran so fast that Dad was airlifted, his body swinging behind his uncle's like a ragdoll. Ashton's fear was so great that he ran straight

---

[24] During a recent conversation with my parents, it became apparent that Aunty Maggie was not the grandmother involved in this story. It was, in fact, "Mama," my father's maternal grandmother who was plagued by this soucouyant. Nonetheless, I decided not to change the story above which, for over thirty years, has been my recollection of my father's story. Even my mother was surprised to learn that Mama, and not Aunty Maggie, was the grandmother at the center of the story. In addition, it apparently was still dark when Mama noticed the blood on the sheet. According to my father, she only was able to see the blood due to the light of a full moon that had shone through the bedroom window. (I told Dad that he had just added that bit for dramatic effect. He said he hadn't.)

[25] Also djablesse or jablesse. Because they are not standardized, creole words in Trinidad often have several spellings.

[26] Fernández Olmos and Paravisini-Gebert also state that in the Caribbean the "world of the spirits includes belief in the sudden apparition of a variety of animal figures in the night sky." Fernández Olmos and Paravisini-Gebert, *Creole Religions of the Caribbean*, 171.

through a closed door.

Recently, my dad told me that these supernatural beings don't exist anymore.

"Why not?" I asked.

"Because there are lights."

"Dad! How you mean none of this exists anymore because of lights?"

"All of these things used to happen under the cover of darkness. With the advent of electricity, a lot of these things have died out."

I didn't quite buy that excuse, although my maternal grandmother once made a similar claim. She said that there's a lot more physical light and enlightenment in the world, so people don't do such things as frequently. That may be true, but I will say that there are many soucouyants still out there—if not literal soucouyants, then metaphorical ones.

Mahal

"Grandma have some good stories, too!" I said to my dad as I climbed into the front passenger seat of his minivan. "I ent know she had so much stories."

I was visiting home from New Orleans, and I'd just finished spending some time with Grandma. Dad picked me up from her house, and as we drove off, I began telling him about all the stories she had told me.

"Like what?" he asked.

"She was tellin' me 'bout some guy who they put obeah on him, and he only goin' 'round de country driving imaginary car."

"Who? Mahal?" my dad asked.

"You know about Mahal, too?!" I said, shocked and a little disappointed.

"Sure. Everybody knows about Mahal. He's a legend."

Although there are several versions of how Mahal came to drive an imaginary car, most claim that he was a witness to a crime and, in order to prevent him from testifying, someone worked obeah on him.

In a 2006 online article in the *Trinidad and Tobago Newsday*, the author begins a story on "bygone characters" with a retelling of the story of Mahal. In this story, Mahal and his sister were the only eyewitnesses to a murder. However, the morning of their court appearance, "the woman woke up staring mad. She believed she was a seamstress and sewed continuously for most of the day on an imaginary sewing machine." Her brother, Mahal, was also afflicted and would spend the rest of his days driving an imaginary motorcar.

> "Will the accused please stand to hear the verdict," the judge said. The murder accused stood up looking more like an athlete about to receive an Olympic gold medal. The judge continued, "Since no witnesses have come forward, the case is dismissed. You may leave the Court." Out in the street, it was noticed that the free man shook the hand of a notorious obeah man.[27]

My grandma's tale differed somewhat from my mom's and from other accounts that I casually perused online after coming home later that afternoon. In her version, Mahal used to transport money for those who worked in the oil fields in the southern portion of the island. He would travel from town to S'ando[28] until one day he was ambushed, and the money—used to pay the oil workers—was stolen. He and his driving companion were to testify at the trial of those accused of the robbery. However, when it was time to take the stand, Mahal wasn't much use to the prosecution.

"He only goin' so," my grandmother said. While sitting at

[27] Unfortunately the name of the author is not listed, though s/he claims that his or her maternal grandmother recounted the story. S/he acknowledges the presence of multiple versions of the story. "Bygone characters," *Trinidad and Tobago Newsday*, Daily News Limited, October 21, 2006, accessed August 16, 2015, http://www.newsday.co.tt/news/0,46367.html.

[28] Trinidadians often refer to Port of Spain as "town" and San Fernando as "S'ando."

the edge of her bed, she made like she was driving a car. Then she got up, turned the wheels of her "imaginary" car and made a right around the corner of the bed. "He goin' so," she gestured.

Mahal's companion was equally useless on the stand. When it was his turn to testify, "He only making like he chucking coconut. He chucking coconut," my grandmother said, as she pretended to use a long pole to get coconuts from a tree.

When my dad and I finally arrived home after driving the short distance from my grandmother's house to ours, no one else was there. I excitedly waited for my mom to arrive so I could tell her about Mahal and the other stories I'd been told.

As soon as she got home, I bombarded her with my newly acquired tale.

"I know 'bout Mahal," she said.

Again, I was a bit disappointed, but there was a twist to my Mahal story, a kicker if you will. Information that neither my mom nor my dad had known previously.

"But guess who was in Prescott Alley?"

"Who? Mahal?" my mom asked excitedly.

"Yes. And Grandma's mom fed him."

My grandmother had begun her story of Mahal's visit to Prescott Alley by telling me how generous her deceased mother, Mercy, was.

"She was always giving, even though she had very little," she said.

One day, Mahal came into the yard in Prescott Alley, weary from travel. He sat down in front their house and requested that my great-grandmother make some food for him. She willingly obliged. Soon, word of Mahal's appearance had spread, and the neighborhood was abuzz with excitement.

"Look! Mahal!" people shouted.

My grandmother's description of Mahal was very similar to other eyewitness accounts that detailed his large calves with protruding veins.

"And he calf big so," she said, looking down at her calf and then up at me while gesturing. She surrounded her calf with both hands, an indication of just how large Mahal's muscle had grown by his incessant walking, excuse me, *driving* around the island.

I told my grandmother that the story of Mahal reminded me of a scene in one of the X-men movies.[29] Towards the end of the film, in the moments before she dies, Wolverine's girlfriend, Kayla Silverfox, a mutant with the power of tactile mind control, condemns a man named Stryker to a lifetime of walking. She tells him, "Walk until your feet bleed, and then keep walking." And that's precisely what he does.

My grandmother nodded her head. "Mind control. That's it. Mind control."

For my grandmother, obeah was very much about mind control. She asked me if I didn't know how in Tobago and in the country people would sometimes find themselves following a light that had no known source. Some would walk all night, and the unluckiest ones would walk themselves off a precipice. Mind control.

* * *

I'm still baffled by the fact that it had taken me over three decades to first hear about the legendary Mahal. How had I not heard of him? My mom never sang any songs about him. And then, my grandmother, who used to call me a badjohn, never once said in reference to my childhood antics, "Yuh mad like Mahal!" But then again, Grandma wouldn't joke about those things. No, I don't think she would joke about obeah and things of a supernatural nature. She knew that those things were no laughing matter.

The Writing on the Wall

The story of Mahal was just one of the stories that my grandmother shared with me that day during my visit to her house. There was one story that I'd heard from my mother on

---

[29] *X-Men Origins: Wolverine*, dir. by Gavin Hood (2009).

several occasions that I specifically asked my grandmother to recount.

According to her, Aunty Elaine's godmother had come to be the guardian of two young children, a girl and a boy. I'm not sure how old they were when she became their caretaker, but my grandmother surmised that during the time of these unfortunate incidents the girl was about fourteen years of age and the boy twelve. Strange things would happen to these children. Their clothes would start to shred as they wore them and would frequently catch fire while being ironed. Perhaps the most frightening of all was the appearance of "bad, evil words" on a wall in the home. One day, Aunty Elaine went to her godmother's house to verify all that she'd heard, and *she self* witnessed foul words being written on the wall by an invisible hand. Eventually, Catholic priests were called. It's not clear exactly what they did, but the evil occurrences stopped.

* * *

Thankfully, my experiences with such supernatural entities have been limited. Like I said before, I regularly pray for protection from such things and I especially pray *not* to see things—*anything*. But sometimes it happens, like it did one day while staying with family in Diego Martin. I stood looking over the balcony of the gallery. Dice, the family dog, was a few feet in front of me, lying down next to the gate, which separated our yard from the neighbor's. After a few moments, I turned my head towards the back of the house, and standing several yards away in front of the washroom was Dice.

"Dice?" I thought to myself.

I turned my head back in the direction of the front of the house, and there she was in the same position as before—lying down next to the gate. And from what I could tell, she had not moved. Confused, but confident that I wasn't crazy, I went inside the house where I saw Ann and decided to tell her of my predicament.

"Strangest thing just happened to me. I was in the gallery, and I saw Dice lying down in the front of the house. Then, I turned towards the back of the house and *I saw Dice*. When I turned my head again, she was lying down in front of the house, in the same position as before. There's no way she could have run to the back of the house and back within the matter of seconds it took for me to turn my head."

Ann's response was very much matter of fact.

"Oh, that's just Blacky, our dog that died. Lots of people see him."

Well, it was as good as any other answer, and so I left it at that. I figured if God was going to let me see any kind of ghost, it would be a ghost dog. I was very fond of dogs after all.

On another occasion, I woke up one morning and again approached Ann with a concern of a supernatural nature.

"Ann, I could have sworn that I heard a male voice call my name—clear as day," I told her.

She said that it was a good thing that I didn't answer; it may have been a bad spirit. Although Ann didn't tell me as much, I have heard others say that by answering the call of an evil spirit one invites death.

Cue: "Jumbie," Scrunter

Not all stories of the supernatural are creepy. Many stories are comical and elicit laughter from deep in one's gut, like the time a neighbor told of a *jumbie*[30] who kept stealing her underwear—that she was wearing!—during the night. And Trinis frequently talk of the spirits that seize them during states of euphoria, like during mas' or while playing an instrument. Phrases like "pan is a jumbie" or "the music just take a hold of me" capture how our greatest feats of creativity come from something outside of us, or maybe from an awakened spirit that was always present.

[30] A jumbie is a ghost or spirit.

This Business of Dreams

[She] begging de boy to try and keep away
Because last night she had a vision
And in the vision he fall in some dirty water
He get a gash but he wouldn't bleed
Right away she know that mean heavy obeah
She sprinkle something, turn 'round, and leave
—"Stick Fight," Anslem Douglas

One of the ways that the supernatural remains present in the lives of Caribbean people is through visions and dreams. This business of dreams is a curious one. So much information comes to us when we seemingly are asleep or when we are wide awake and having thoughts and seeing images that go beyond mere daydreaming. The knowledge that I have garnered from my own dreams is one of the reasons that I cannot help but believe in a higher power. As I've gotten older, I've learned to distinguish between dreams that are prophetic and those that are based on the last television show I watched the night before. One of the scariest, and most memorable, prophetic dreams I've had consisted of a house fire—in our house. Well, not exactly our house. We live in what is known as a "semi-attached" house; we share a wall with the neighbors to our left. I dreamt that there was a fire in our neighbor's house that spread to ours. The following day, as I was walking home from the subway, I turned the corner and saw a fire truck stationed in front of my home. I quickened my pace and hurried down the block. I was somewhat relieved when I realized that the fire was across the street. I never quite understood the purpose of the dream, other than perhaps to make me heed the signs and signals that I get in life.

Dreams may serve as warnings, but they also serve to provide messages of comfort from those living beyond the grave.

* * *

A woman kept visiting my great-aunt, "Boonty," in her dreams. Boonty didn't recognize the woman haunting her, but described her as a short Spanish woman, her hair neatly tied back in a ponytail. The woman carried a bible and a candle, and she kept assuring Boonty that everything would be all right; my great-aunt would survive the cancer.

"But who is this woman who keeps coming to me in a dream?" Boonty found herself wondering time and time again.

One day, she recounted these reoccurring dreams to a cousin who replied, "You en't even know yuh own family. The woman is your great-grandmother."

Boonty's great-grandmother was sending her a message of faith and love from the other side. And the woman in her dreams, my great-great-great-grandmother, was right. Boonty did survive the cancer, and we're all glad she did.

Being in this World

For many Caribbean people, learning to observe signs and signals is a part of being in this world, regardless of one's religious affiliation. Nonetheless, it took me a long time to realize that we don't all experience signs and signals in the same way or receive them with the same frequency.

* * *

My heart started pounding. I wanted to get up and hit somebody. Then I realized it was that girl. I'd never seen her before. She had stepped onto the train at the last stop and had sat down across from me. The anger and bitterness that flowed through her body passed from her to me, and it took every bit of my being not to fly into a rage. There was an empty seat at the other end of the subway car. I promptly got up and moved.

It took a while for me to recognize that I would "catch" other people's moods, but I've always been aware of my keen dislike for being near to or touched by certain people. I vividly remember a pastor stretching out his hand to shake mine when I was a child—maybe nine or ten years old. I wouldn't extend my hand to him. I later told my dad that he was "the spawn of the Devil."

"You mustn't say such things," my father replied.

Years later, that pastor would be the cause of much stress in my father's life.

By the time I graduated from college, I became acutely aware of my heightened sensitivity to people and my penchant for not only seeing through the masks people wear, but also sometimes taking on their physical, mental, and emotional states as my own. I realized that I had been "reading" people ever since I was a child. I remember looking at children and adults as I rode the bus with my mom and predicting with much confidence their future lives. "He will be a doctor," I'd think to myself, or "Oh no. He is going to end up in jail." As I got older, if a friend told me about a new romantic interest, I'd ask for the person's name, and based on that information, I would sometimes make an assessment of that person's character—not based on the name, but on the vibe I got from the person's name in that moment. I don't remember a time my assessment was wrong. This was nothing that I tried to do or even thought about explicitly. And it never occurred to me that many people don't experience the world in the same way.

Annoyingly, I sometimes acquire the physical pain of others—nothing too severe, but enough of a nuisance for me to go to the doctor. Later (sometimes months later!), I'll find out that someone close to me has been suffering with an illness in the area of my body that's been afflicted, and my symptoms suddenly disappear. At other times, I have found myself in despair—for no reason. On such occasions, it is easy to snap myself out of an emotional state by simply recognizing (and usually saying out loud), "This is not me." However, it is much more difficult for me to separate myself from the difficult emotional states of others if I am also going through something.

What do we call this "ability"? Quite frankly, I never gave it a name. And as I've said, for many years, I was not even aware that this ability existed. It has been called many names by many people, some of whom have different belief systems. Some would label me an intuitive, a psychic, an empath, or an intercessor with "spiritual gifts." Others might just call me a witch. Whatever terminology one would like to employ, it is simply another facet of my life.

* * *

Maybe it's this heightened awareness and sensitivity to people that has instilled in me a desire to always dig beneath the surface of appearances and to seek out the truth of a matter. I take very few things at face value, and I know that in getting to know a person or a culture, one has to critically engage with not just that person or culture, but with the information presented about them.

Chapter 5:

The Empire Strikes

But as I began to get into the history of the music, I found that this was impossible without, at the same time, getting deeper into the history of the people. That it was the history of the Afro-American people as text, as tale, as story, as exposition, narrative, or what have you, that the music was the score, the actually expressed creative orchestration, reflection, of Afro-American life, our words, the libretto, to those actual, lived lives. That the music was an orchestrated, vocalized, hummed, chanted, blown, beaten, scatted, corollary confirmation of the history. And that one could go from one to the other, actually, from the inside to the outside, or reverse, and be talking about the same things. That the music was explaining the history as the history was explaining the music. And that both were expressions of and reflections of the people!

—Excerpt from Blues People, Leroi Jones[1]

When I think of the Caribbean

It was the second class of the semester. In the previous class we had already done our introductions and syllabus review for the course I was teaching, "Caribbean Music." Today was when the fun would begin. I took off the cap of a black dry erase marker and proceeded to write on the board in my best penmanship:

"When I think of the Caribbean, I think of..."

---

[1] Leroi Jones (Amiri Baraka), *Blues People: Negro Music in White America*, (New York, London, Toronto, Sydney: Harper Perennial, 1999), ix-x.

It was a prompt, designed to help me (and my students) ascertain the extent of their prior knowledge on the Caribbean. In addition to that first prompt, I wrote down several more specific ones which implored students to write down what came to mind when they thought of various words in association with the Caribbean: landscape, countries, food, language, people, race, religion, music, literature, and history.

After taking a few minutes to write, my students and I discussed their responses as a class.

"When I think of Caribbean countries, I think of…? What did you write down?" I asked. Students raised their hands to speak or shouted out their answers.

"Jamaica."

"Cuba."

"And what foods come to mind when you think of the Caribbean?"

"Jerk chicken."

"Roti."

"What kinds of music do you associate with the Caribbean?"

"Reggae."

"Steel drums."

These were just a handful of their responses, and in general, my students could rattle off a list of countries, food, and music genres associated with the Caribbean. However, I am never surprised, and I am always disappointed, that my students never have much to say about the history of the Caribbean and even less about its literature.

Over the course of the two years that I taught Caribbean Music, my classes were small, roughly 10-15 students. Despite their size, these classes were exceptionally diverse, disproportionately so when compared to the university as a whole. I had a few students from the Caribbean or with Caribbean roots, a few white American students, and two or three students of Asian descent, at least one of whom was an international student. My class could be the poster-child for diversity.

I've always known that music is a very powerful expression, one that has the power to bring seemingly different people together. That was the reason that I decided to study and teach music. But it became evident to me that it would take more than a shared love of music to bridge the many chasms that separate people. It would also take more than teaching music history and culture to a diverse group of students. A statement made by rapper and businessman Jay Z for Oprah's *Master Class* will help to illuminate some of my concerns.

> I think that hip hop has done more for racial relations than most cultural icons…save Martin Luther King, because his dream speech we realized when President Obama got elected. But, the impact of the music, you know, this music didn't only influence kids from urban areas. It influenced people all around the world… It's very difficult to teach racism when your kid looks up to Snoop Doggy Dogg. And if you look at clubs and how integrated they have become, before people partied in separate clubs. There were hip hop clubs and there were techno clubs, and now people party together. And once you have people partying, dancing, and singing along to the same music, then conversations naturally happen after that, right? And then within conversations…we all realize that we're more alike than we're separate.[2]

Jay Z took a lot of heat on social media for his commentary, which suggests that hip hop has done more for race relations in the U.S. than "most cultural icons…save Martin Luther King." His uncritical assessment is problematic on several levels, but I'll briefly tackle a few of them.

1. Dr. King's speech has not been realized. There is nothing in his speech that states that his dream would come to fruition when a black man was elected presi-

[2] "Jay-Z on Race: 'We're More Alike Than We're Separate' | Master Class | Oprah Winfrey Network," YouTube video, 2:00, posted by "OWN," January 4, 2015, https://www.youtube.com/watch?v=OiF2oKfFQTQ.

dent of the United States.
2. The music of black America has a history of influence throughout the world, from blues to jazz to rock and roll, etc. And these musics went global in an age that was not as technologically advanced as the one in which hip hop emerged and in which it currently exists.
3. It is a fallacy to imply that clubs are integrated because of hip hop. Rather there were "cultural icons" and many lesser-known people of various races who risked their lives to integrate spaces and dismantle Jim Crow. If black and white bodies are dancing together at hip hop concerts, it's because they can. Had it not been for the Civil Rights Movement, Jay Z might have had to perform separate concerts for blacks and whites and even enter through back entrances to the places where he performed.
4. And finally, conversations don't necessarily occur naturally from occupying the same space, especially those conversations that honestly tackle difficult topics like race.

What fascinates me about Jay Z's response is that I could easily hear his statement come out of the mouths of several of my students. At best, it's a naïve and ignorant way in which to view the world. But, as they say, "ignorance is bliss." At worst, it reduces racial progress to superficial symbols of unity.[3]

Part of the antidote to the types of uncritical thinking that afflicts all of us on some level is not only to learn more about the history of the music, but also be able to think about that history critically. But knowing the history is not enough; one also needs to truly (not superficially) understand the people and culture behind the music.

---

[3] It is particularly easy in this technological age for us to feel like we "get" another culture, and that we are making racial progress, simply because we can share the music, food, and other aspects of a culture, even though we may never actually engage with the people of that culture on a personal level.

* * *

Music is one of our greatest teachers, or at least it has the potential to be. In the introduction to his book *Blues People: Negro Music in White America*, Amiri Baraka, writing as Leroi Jones, states that the blues "was the history of the Afro-American people," a "reflection, of Afro-American life."[4] Though writing specifically on the descendants of enslaved Africans brought to the United States, Baraka's words describe the relationship between history, music, and the many other cultural products of African-descended people the world over.

That the music explains the history, and the history explains the music, has never been lost on me. After all, I grew up with my mother giving me history lessons through song. However, it increasingly became apparent to me, especially as I grew older, that knowledge of the music does not necessarily mean that one will comprehend the socio-historical lessons contained within. Furthermore, in today's world, where cultural products are borrowed, shared, and appropriated at an increasingly fast pace, sometimes the music is changed to such an extent that the lesson is trivialized or worse, rendered invisible. I hoped that in my classes students would realize that one cannot fully understand a music without understanding the history of the people making that music.

The sounds of the Caribbean offer lessons in the historical lives of its people. Unfortunately, for many people who live outside of the region, learning those lessons has been hampered by perceptions of the Caribbean as a sort of tourist paradise. In his book *Silencing the Past: Power and the Production of History*, anthropologist Michel-Rolph Trouillot states that "most Europeans and North Americans learn their first history lessons through media that have not been subjected to the standards set by peer reviews, university presses, or doctoral committees."[5] For many, particularly Eu-

---

[4] Baraka, *Blues People*, ix.

[5] Michel-Rolph Trouillot, *Silencing the Past: Power and the Production of History* (Boston: Beacon Press, 1995), 20.

ropeans and North Americans, tourism advertisements and kitschy or exotic album covers have meant that the word "Caribbean" evokes images of white sandy beaches, the sounds of "steel drums," and the smiling faces of locals. People think of reggae and Bob Marley and of Harry Belafonte and the "Banana Boat Song."

"Rum and Coca-Cola," one of the most iconic songs of the post-WWII era, succinctly demonstrates how the Caribbean (and in this case, specifically Trinidad) has been romanticized to U.S. audiences.

If you ever go down Trinidad
They make you feel so very glad
Calypso sing and make up rhyme
Guarantee you one real good fine time
—"Rum and Coca-Cola," The Andrews Sisters

Cue: "Rum and Coca-Cola," The Andrews Sisters

Recorded by the Andrews Sisters in 1944, the hit song functions almost as an advertisement for Trinidad and Tobago's Ministry of Tourism. It portrays Trinidad as a highly enjoyable place where the people and culture are guaranteed to give visitors "one good fine time." However, I find most interesting the ways in which the song depicts the presence of U.S. soldiers on the island—a result of World War II—as benevolent. Yankee soldiers are presented in a rather positive light, as the "young girls say they treat 'em nice, [and] make Trinidad like paradise." All the while they are:

Drinkin' rum and Coca-Cola
Go down Point Cumana
Both mother and daughter
Workin' for the Yankee dollar

Life is like a fantasy on the island where the "native girls all dance and smile" from "Chica-chick-carry to Monos Isle."[6] Furthermore, the allure of the American soldiers is too strong for the local "native peach" who makes "tropic love" with her G.I.; the following day they "sit in hot sun and cool off." As sung by the Andrews Sisters, the song arguably plays into stereotypes about the Caribbean and its people as well as unflappable images of U.S. soldiers stationed in "exotic" locales.

For many Americans, the Caribbean is precisely the paradise alluded to in the lyrics above. Yet, the portrayal of the Caribbean in this song is an illusion. The reality is that, below the surface, the people of the Caribbean have experienced economic and social upheaval at the hands of several European nations and the United States through centuries of colonialism and imperialism. Belinda Edmonson refers to this discrepancy between the lived reality of Caribbean people and that which is actually portrayed in public and academic discourses as the "romance" of the Caribbean, that is, "idealized representations of Caribbean society."[7] Edmondson's use of the word "romance" "draws on what Northrop Frye has called the 'vulgar sense of the word'—that is, a sentimentalized or rose-colored view of reality—because the idealized is inevitably sentimentalized."[8] Furthermore, Frye states that a defining aspect of romance is "its effort to maintain a self-consistent idealized world without the intrusions of realism or irony."[9]

---

[6] There are several islands in the Caribbean Sea that are under the sovereignty of Trinidad and Tobago, including the islands of Chacachacare (pronounced incorrectly as CHICA-CHICK-CARRY in the song) and Monos. Locals refer to visits to these islands as "going down the islands." Historically, the islands were frequented by wealthy Trinidadians of predominantly European heritage.

[7] Belinda Edmonson, "Introduction: The Caribbean: Myths, Tropes, Discourses," in *Caribbean Romances: The Politics of Regional Representation*, ed. Belinda Edmondson (Charlottesville and London: University Press of Virginia, 1999), 2.

[8] Ibid.

[9] Ibid., 3.

It is precisely this lack of realism and irony that is missing from "Rum and Coca-Cola," as sung by the Andrews Sisters. When I think of the Caribbean, I think of much more than tourism advertisements and notions of "fun in the sun" while drinking "rum and Coca-Cola."[10] I think of my family and the legacy they have bequeathed to me—the music, the food, and all aspects of Trinbagonian culture. When I think of the Caribbean, I think of the steelpan and how those panmen were once outcasts in their own country, and how their journey toward respectability came in part because of their acceptance abroad in Europe and "America." For me, steelpan does not symbolize a tourist's paradise. It symbolizes an ingenuity that flew in the face of the oppression of a group of people, a repression of their way of life and of their ways of being. It represents how from a ban on drumming emerged the tamboo bamboo and eventually the "magic" hidden within a "rusty old drum."[11] It symbolizes overcoming the notion that a *wutless*,[12] colonized people could never amount to anything, never do anything with purpose. Steelpan is colonialism, imperialism, poverty, and crime alchemized into love.

I think of Bob Marley and reggae, and how the Rasta faith has been defanged in this country by those who would represent it as merely dreadlocks and marijuana. Its roots in Marcus Garvey's Universal Negro Improvement Association (U.N.I.A.) and its focus on black empowerment go unnoticed, but not by me. When I think of the Caribbean, I think also of the immigrants in my neighborhood, throughout the United States, and across the globe. I think of the struggles that these immigrants face in their new home, especially those who are living abroad undocumented. And I think of all the reasons that they may have had for leaving family and friends to make

---

[10] Note that I said that I think about more than those things. Yes, I think of beaches and palm trees, but my relationship to the landscape is very different than that of your average tourist.

[11] "Make magic from old steel, from rusty old drum." From Denyse Plummer's calypso, "Nah Leaving."

[12] Worthless.

a life and a living for themselves in a strange land. I think of a history of migration steeped in violence and empire, a history which informs the present and which has yet to be overcome. I think of all these things because I know the history. Immigrants have an awareness that others often lack, an awareness of the world beyond their front door, an understanding of the complexities of this world based on having lived in places that are often vastly different from one another. People outside of the United States and Europe are all too aware of how colonialism and imperialism have worked to the detriment of their homelands. People are generally aware of those who have more power than them, especially those who have power *over* them. It is a survival instinct.

Immigrants are particularly aware when history is being sanitized. Granted, it is not uncommon for life to be portrayed in an idealized fashion in artist renderings or tourist brochures. As such, the illusion presented to the American public in the form of "Rum and Coca-Cola" by the Andrews Sisters may not have been so problematic had there not already existed a song by the same name, with essentially the same melody, and quite a different story to tell. Imagine the surprise of one Rupert Grant, also known as Lord Invader, when he heard the Andrews Sisters singing a song that he had written and popularized in Trinidad. The original "Rum and Coca-Cola" told a much different story than the version sung by the Andrews Sisters. In his song, Lord Invader creates a portrait of American soldiers disrupting the social fabric of the island by encouraging prostitution and luring women away from their husbands and/or local clients.[13]

On the record, *Calypso at Midnight!*,[14] Lord Invader is asked if he could speak a little about calypso and how it is that

[13] And though love stories undoubtedly emerged between local women and U.S. soldiers wherever they have been stationed, there are other sides to the story, ones that do not depict U.S. soldiers in such a nice light.

[14] Recorded in 1946 by folklorist and ethnomusicologist Alan Lomax, the album contains live performances of several popular calypsonians during a concert given at Town Hall in New York City.

he came to compose the lyrics to "Rum and Coca-Cola." His response is telling.

> Calypso is a folklore of Trinidad. A style of poetry telling about current events in song…I was traveling on a bus to someplace they call Point Cumana—bathing resort—and I happened to see the G.I.s, *since the American social invasion in the West Indies, Trinidad [laughter].* You know the girls used to get their candies and stuff like [laughter] that and they go out to the canteens with the boys and so on and have fun. So I notice since the G.I.s came over there that we generally chase with soda, ordinary soda. But their chaser was rum and Coke. They drink rum and they like the Coca-Cola as a chaser. So I study that as an idea of song, and Morey Amsterdam[15] had the nerve to say that he composed that song back here. Thank you ladies and gentlemen.[16]

It is interesting to note that Invader's mention of "the American social invasion" in Trinidad elicited laughter. Perhaps he made a gesture that would better qualify his statement. (After all, calypsonians are known for employing double entendres and coded messages that sometimes are most clearly made evident through performance.) However, I'd argue that there is much seriousness behind those words, which I think is fully supported by the original lyrics of the song.

Cue: "Rum and Coca-Cola," "Yankee Dollar," Lord Invader; "Jean and Dinah," Mighty Sparrow

Lord Invader's "Rum and Coca-Cola" is about more than just a popular alcoholic beverage. The first line of the song

---

[15] Morey Amsterdam was a comedian, actor, and television personality most known for his role as "Buddy Sorrell" on *The Dick Van Dyke Show.*

[16] Lord Invader, "Introduction to Rum and Coca-Cola," *Calypso at Midnight!,* comp. Alan Lomax, Rounder Select, 1999, compact disc. Emphasis mine.

hints that the relationship between the Yankee soldiers and women discussed is not romantic but contractual, as the Yankees "give them a better price."

And when the Yankees first went to Trinidad
Some of the young girls were more than glad
They said that the Yankees treat them nice
And they give them a better price

While the untrained or puritanical ear might just as well assume that the Yankees are simply paying more for innocuous goods and services, in Trinidad and other parts of the Caribbean people grow up learning how to read between the lines. Coded messages in the form of *double entendres* and innuendos are important rhetorical devices in the African tradition that have been retained in the Trinidad calypso and other musics from the African diaspora. The implication is clear; these women—mothers and daughters—are "working" as prostitutes for the Yankee dollar.[17]

Lord Invader's "Rum and Coca-Cola" is not the only song to tackle U.S. imperialism in Trinidad. His song "Yankee Dollar" also examines the effect of the U.S. presence (i.e., the "American social invasion") on male-female relationships in Trinidad. In the song, Lord Invader loses his girlfriend from a respectable family to a Yankee soldier who was treating her "much better." He sings:

So she told me plainly
She love Yankee money
And she said, "Lord Invader,
Not because you sang 'Rum and Coca-Cola'
Don't bother if you know you ent got that Yankee dollar"

[17] Again, live performances of calypsos often provide clues to the double meanings contained within lyrics.

In many ways, this song, recorded in 1946,[18] foreshadows the popular "Jean and Dinah" by the Mighty Sparrow, as Lord Invader describes how the end of the war and softening of the U.S. presence in Trinidad negatively impacted local women.

But now the war is over
Trinidad is getting harder
Some of the women bawling for murder
And you can hear dem how they gossiping
No more Yankee dollars they spending and thing
But now they hustling for they usual shilling

A decade later, Sparrow's "Jean and Dinah," more explicitly tackles the subject of prostitution while American soldiers were stationed in Trinidad. Sparrow's commentary is decidedly more harsh than both "Rum and Coca-Cola" and "Yankee Dollar." The calypsonian does not suggest that (even some of) the local men in his song are jilted boyfriends and husbands. Rather, they are former "Johns," or customers, of the local prostitutes who, upon the declining presence of the U.S. military in Trinidad, are "out for revenge" on the women who ignored them while they catered to the wealthy (at least by comparison) U.S. servicemen.

It's the glamour boys again
We are going to rule Port of Spain
No more Yankees to spoil the fête
Dorothy have to take what she get
All of them who used to make style
Well they taking two shilling with a smile
No more hotel to rest your head
By the sweat of thy brow thou shall eat bread

The last line, which borrows from the Bible, is especially harsh,

---

[18] See John Cowley, liner notes to *Calypso in New York*, Lord Invader, Smithsonian Folkways Recordings SFW CD 40454, 2000, compact disc.

particularly within the context of prostitution.[19]

Both Lord Invader's "Rum and Coca-Cola" and Sparrow's "Jean and Dinah" paint a picture of the U.S. presence in Trinidad that is messier and a lot less romantic than Morey Amsterdam would have had the American public believe. As such, it is likely that Lord Invader's version of "Rum and Coca-Cola" would not have been as successful as the one by the Andrews Sisters because it does not portray the U.S. positively and tackles the issue of U.S. imperialism. I suspect that "Jean and Dinah" would have fared worse, and to my knowledge, while an enduring hit in Trinidad, it was never remade for mass consumption in the United States.

Is a Song Just a Song?

Cue: "Boom Up History," "Talk Yuh Talk," 3 Canal

Does it really matter that the Andrews Sisters' version of "Rum and Coca-Cola" portrays a romanticized image of U.S. servicemen stationed in Trinidad? After all, there were truly romantic liaisons between the G.I.s and local women. Had the song not been a remake of an already socio-political song, I might be inclined to say no. However, the theft and de-politicization of a song critical of Americans for consumption by Americans is problematic if only because of the power differentials between the U.S. and Trinidad and the role of the media in maintaining such hierarchies.

Earlier I mentioned that, according to anthropologist Michel-Rolph Trouillot, "most Europeans and North Americans learn their first history lessons through media."[20] As such, the theft and popularization of the Andrews Sisters' version over the original is an example of history in blackface—those in power co-opting the lived realities of a group of people and

---

[19] Genesis 3:19 (King James Version)—"In the sweat of thy face shalt thou eat bread, till thou return unto the ground; for out of it wast thou taken: for dust thou art, and unto dust shalt thou return."

[20] Trouillot, *Silencing the Past*, 20.

re-presenting them as not just fact, but truth. It is an example of history being told by those who won. In *Silencing the Past*, Trouillot makes the following poignant statement:

> Silences enter the process of historical production at four crucial moments: the moment of fact creation (the making of *sources*); the moment of fact assembly (the making of *archives*); the moment of fact retrieval (the making of *narratives*); and the moment of retrospective significance (the making of *history* in the final instance).[21]

The Andrews Sisters' "Rum and Coca-Cola" was a huge hit in the United States even though it was banned, not for a discussion of prostitution (which clearly went over many heads), but for its promotion of alcohol and its mention of a brand name product. Nonetheless, it undoubtedly made an impact as it remained at the top of the *Billboard* charts for several weeks. It thus became a *source* of information about Trinidad (and the greater Caribbean region) for a large section of the U.S. population, and it contributed to a *narrative* of a benevolent U.S. military and "happy go-lucky" living in the Caribbean. As Trouillot explains, there is an intimate relationship between history and power, evident in the fact that "the production of historical narratives involves the uneven contribution of competing groups and individuals who have unequal access to the means for such production."[22] Although Lord Invader successfully sued Morey Amsterdam for copyright infringement, the Andrews Sisters' version of "Rum and Coca-Cola" has remained more popular than the original and thus has had a wider influence in shaping the narrative regarding the U.S. presence in Trinidad.

The irony is that when the Andrews Sisters' version was released, Jim Crow was in effect in the United States; inter-

[21] Ibid., 26. Author's emphasis.

[22] Ibid., xix.

racial marriage was not yet legal throughout the country.[23] It really leads one to think about how and why the portrayal of interracial unions in the Andrews Sisters' version was tolerated by the American public. Was there any backlash against the song on those grounds? If not, why not? How is it okay to enjoy the cultural products of a country but despise its people in your own country? The concern for me is that the song then becomes part of an insidious (albeit perhaps unconscious) narrative whereby black and brown women are acceptable as vessels with which to play out the erotic fantasies of white males, while being denied basic civil rights.[24] After all, the romantic fantasy depicted in the Andrews Sisters' version would not have taken place in the U.S. during the 1940s without considerable backlash.

These power relations aren't solely black versus white or Western versus non-Western, to use common dichotomies. There are many untold stories that "Rum and Coca-Cola," "Yankee Dollar," and "Jean and Dinah" allude to but never address. For example, what of the romantic relationships that did form between Trinidadian women and U.S. soldiers? What are the stories of those couples and their offspring? And I am most interested in the stories of the women portrayed in these songs. Lord Invader portrays Trinidadian women as gold diggers and prostitutes, and the Mighty Sparrow specifically targets prostitutes in his song in ways that suggest that these "working girls" owe fidelity to Trinidadian men, despite their profession being a capitalist enterprise. What story would a calypso (or calypsos) told through their eyes tell? What new information would it add to the picture, and how would it alter our understanding of history?

---

[23] The 1967 Supreme Court decision in the case of Loving v. Virginia made anti-miscegenation laws illegal in the U.S.

[24] This was certainly the case under slavery, where black women were raped by white men (i.e. acceptable sexual vessels), but denied human and civil rights.

Cue: "Slave," Mighty Sparrow

The question of whose story gets told is an important one, and one that has been afflicting people throughout the Americas since Columbus' first voyage. Imagine my horror when encountering the following situation while attending a pre-wedding event for a friend's upcoming nuptials. The grandmother of the groom lived in a quaint house in New England that was about as old as the nation. It was a beautiful and kempt house and exuded historical charm. At some point in the evening, the elderly owner of the house (who I believe had had too much alcohol) approached me and said something to this effect:

"Our family had slaves, and they liked us so much that they stayed with us even after slavery ended."

One of the other attendees (a young white woman with blond hair and blue eyes, no less) looked like she was going to explode with rage. Better her than me.[25] Clearly upset, the young woman apologized for the unnecessary and untimely words of the homeowner. The homeowner's granddaughter, who seemed to only catch part of my interaction with her grandmother, replied:

"I'm not sure exactly what was said, but I apologize."

Had she been a younger person, I might have exchanged words with the older woman. However, in some cases, I don't believe you can teach old dogs new tricks, and there was no point raising my blood pressure and spoiling my friend's party over this nonsense. Yet this was not the first time I had heard the notion that former slaves remaining in the homes of their former masters was an indication of good relations between these two groups, as opposed to a survival strategy on the part of the formerly enslaved. I think of the Mighty Sparrow singing of the plight of some Afro-Trinidadians following emancipation.

I was then put out on the street
I have no clothes

---

[25] One must always be aware of feeding into the "angry black woman" stereotype.

I have no food
I've no place to sleep

Hmm...I had no education
No particular ambition
This I cannot conceal

Forgot my native culture
Live like a vulture
From the white man I had to steal![26]

What Sparrow's song might encourage someone to consider is that many former slaves would not refuse to continue living in the homes of their "masters," especially if the alternative was to try and survive without basic needs. So while some left the plantation, others remained, as that choice represented their best mode of survival.[27]

And it is plausible that emancipated slaves had a good enough relationship with their owners to warrant staying with them. I can buy that. However, if the terms "slave" and "owner" were replaced with the words "captive" and "kidnapper," we would call that situation "Stockholm Syndrome." It is this syndrome that afflicts the notorious figure of Uncle Tom and arguably most of the formerly enslaved (and their descendants) to some degree. By asserting and privileging a narrative that posits that living with "former" slave masters was an indication of good relationships between enslaved and master, we are presenting a rose-colored view of the aftermath of slavery that not only deemphasizes the brutality of slavery and its

[26] Mighty Sparrow, "Slave."

[27] Be aware that the post-emancipation situation was different in different parts of the Americas. Slavery ended in certain countries much later than in others. And while difficult in most countries, I would venture to say that the terrorism faced by the formerly enslaved in the United States was among the most horrifically inhumane. I generally don't like to compare "suffering"; however, the situation in the U.S. was unlike many other parts of the Americas particularly due to the failure of Reconstruction, the implementation of Jim Crow laws, and the real and psychological torture of black bodies through lynching, sterilizations, etc.

psychological effects, but actually humanizes the slave master while dehumanizing the formerly enslaved.

Former slave masters (and by extension, their descendants) are humanized in the sense that they are permitted to have a range of human attitudes and experiences. They can enslave and terrorize a group of people yet still be considered kind and caring individuals on some level. On the other hand, the formerly enslaved (and by extension, their descendants) are not afforded that opportunity. After enduring generations of slavery, they were expected to continue working side by side with their oppressors without feelings of disgust, distrust, and disaffection for those who had not only kept them and their ancestors in captivity for generations, but also continued to oppress them in the "post-emancipation" era. In our society, only animals are expected to be held hostage and remain loyal to their captors.

I can never be certain why this elderly woman felt the need to broach the topic of slavery with me at this party. My family didn't even experience slavery in this country, so seeking absolution from me was futile. I suppose she either was trying to cover up for her latent racism and/or she genuinely felt guilty that her family had owned slaves. Regardless, approaching the only black person at the party with that nonsense just illustrates how uncomfortable many people still are when dealing with the history and legacy of slavery in this country. I suspect that part of this discomfort with the topics of slavery and race comes from the concern that if the story were told in its entirety, black people would *rightly* seek, and be allowed to seek, retribution for past injustices, resulting in wealth redistribution in the U.S.

Dr. Hollis Liverpool, who also goes by the sobriquet the "Mighty Chalkdust," once said, "You have to be a big person to learn history."[28] By this he meant that there are a lot of things in history to make a person uneasy, so one has to have a certain amount of maturity, courage, and objectivity to look into the past. I would add that one also has to have those same

[28] Spoken during a class lecture given at Trinity College in Hartford, CT.

qualities in order to look at how the past (still) informs the present, particularly with issues pertaining to race.

Race and Ethnicity

Say it loud! I'm black and I'm proud!
—"Say It Loud —I'm Black & I'm Proud," James Brown

Regardless of its dubious roots in biology, race is real because, to paraphrase W. I. Thomas, people act as though it is real and thus it has become real in its consequences.
—Philip Kasinitz, *Caribbean New York*[29]

Cue: "Say It Loud—I'm Black and I'm Proud," James Brown; "Black is Beautiful," Mighty Duke; "Split Me in Two," Mighty Dougla; "African," Brother Superior

My dad always likes to joke, "I'm not black. I'm Brown," a clear play on race, color, and our last name. I always thanked God that I was just brown, plain old brown. Not too light and not too dark. I've seen how colorism—prejudice based on skin tone—has operated within communities of color. I've heard dark-skinned girls say that they would not be friends with girls lighter than the color of a brown paper bag, and I've heard light-skinned girls belittle their darker sisters precisely because of their skin tone.

One of my earliest memories of "colorism" within the black community occurred one day while attending school at Emma Lazarus. I was in the fourth grade, and about eight or nine years old, when the incident occurred. I can't be certain, but I believe that my class was having lunch, as I remember passing through a corridor that connected the school cafeteria to another part of the building. I'm not sure where I was going,

[29] Kasinitz, *Caribbean New York*, 4.

but as I walked through the hallway, I unwittingly stumbled upon an in-progress feud. One of my classmates, Natalie,[30] was apparently involved in a spat with another child when I heard her say five words that have remained with me for almost thirty years.

"That's why you so *black*!"

The words flowed out of her mouth with the assuredness of a girl who just *knew* she had had the last word. Although I witnessed the event, I'm not even sure who Natalie was arguing with or why. I do know I remember the bitterness with which she hurled that "insult" at another classmate. The words Natalie said that day—they stung my ears; they still do.

If that wasn't bad enough, I was enveloped by a wave of embarrassment when a white woman, one of the school aides, stopped Natalie to explain to her the inappropriateness of what she had said. Although I have always been grateful to that woman for having the moral fiber to stop this child and teach her that her actions were wrong, I have never felt good about a white woman having to tell a black child not to spew racial venom towards another black child. However, the legacy of slavery, colonialism, and imperialism in the Americas (and elsewhere) did not just influence black/white relations; it continuously affects interactions among people from and descended from Africa and Asia, the ways in which they perceive themselves, and the ways in which they are perceived by others.

"You're pretty for a dark-skinned girl."

"He's so black and ugly."

"She thinks she's all that 'cause she light-skinned."

And on, and on, and on. I've heard it all. Friends who since childhood have been made to feel inferior because of their dark skin tone and kinky hair. Other friends who were ostracized because their adolescent peers didn't want to be friends with a probably stuck-up girl with light skin and "good hair."

Thankfully, I haven't internalized negative perceptions of

---

[30] Natalie is a pseudonym for my former classmate.

others based on skin color, at least not to that extent. As I like to say, "I'm an equal opportunity hater," but perhaps that's because my parents never used skin color as the basis for an insult and/or not liking someone. Maybe that's because many of the women in my immediate family are dark-skinned, including my mom, Grandma, and Aunty Ruby. (And we already know that my mom thinks she's "hot stuff.") Maybe it's because in our home in Brooklyn, race and ethnicity were freely discussed in conversations about prejudice, racism, and self-hatred.

Racial prejudice and colorism are facets of life in Trinidad too, a country where the majority of the population consists of people descended from Africa and Asia. Again, you'll find these issues virtually anywhere colonialism and imperialism reared its head. And again, Mom would have songs appropriate to the discussion. She had the perfect song for depicting some of the racial tensions that had emerged in Trinidad, where British colonialism resulted in Africans and Asians living side by side and eventually having mixed race children, known locally as *douglas.* Mom would sing the chorus of "Split Me in Two," a song by the Mighty Dougla, who, as evident by his name, is of mixed African and Indian descent.

Because they sending Indians to India
And the Negroes back to Africa
Can somebody please just tell me
Where they sending poor me
I am neither one nor the other
Six a one, half a dozen of the other
If they serious 'bout sending back people for true
They bound to split me in two

In this song, the Mighty Dougla humorously describes the plight of being a dougla in Trinidad. The song opens with a hypothetical situation. "Let us suppose they pass a law. They don't want people living here anymore." It is decided that Trinidadians would have "to find their country, according to [their] race originally." The Mighty Dougla finds himself in a predicament. Being of mixed race, where would he go?

The song continues with the calypsonian describing his inability to find playmates as a child; neither black nor Indian children wanted to play with him. And as he got older he found himself on the wrong side of racial strife, attacked by blacks for being Indian and by Indians for being black. "Dougie" describes having the misfortune of walking past "some Indians and Negroes rioting" when:

> *A Indian man cuff me straight in me face*
> *I ran by the Negroes to get rescue*
> *"Look ah coolie!" and them start beating me too*

Though the song is humorous, the pain of the dougla is palpable. Although the Mighty Dougla doesn't discuss the meaning of the term, anyone who knows its origins will understand how until the latter part of the 20th century, to be a dougla was to be an anomaly and not necessarily welcomed with open arms. In "The *Dougla* in Trinidad's Consciousness," Ferne Louanne Regis writes:

> *Douglas*, the offspring of Indo-African unions, occupy an ambiguous position in Trinidadian society. Etymologically, the word *Dougla* is linked to *dogla* which is of Indic origin and is defined by Platts (1884, 534) as "a person of impure breed, a hybrid, a mongrel; a two-faced or deceitful person and a hypocrite." In Bihar, Northern India, from where many Indian indentured labourers migrated to Trinidad, *dogla* still carries the meaning of a person of impure breed related specifically to the "progeny of inter-varna marriage, acquiring the connotation of 'bastard', meaning illegitimate son of a prostitute, only in a secondary sense" (Reddock 1994, 101). We do not know how and when the term *Dougla* became equated to the offspring of Indian-African unions in Trinidad but we may surmise

> that it originated in traditional Indian contempt for the darker-skinned (Brereton 1974, 24).[31]

Although the term *dougla* generally is not perceived as a derogatory term in Trinidad today, its origins suggest that the word was invoked to disparage the offspring of Trinidadians of African and Indian descent. And indeed, as demonstrated in the song, Afro-Indo relations in Trinidad have not always been easy.

In contrast to "Split Me in Two," where the protagonist struggles with his mixed race identity, my mother offered another song on the topic of race for consideration, one that generated considerable debate amongst her family when it was released in Trinidad.

"No matter where yuh born, yuh still African," she would sing.

It was an interesting statement, one that had our family in Brooklyn discussing its veracity.

If an Indian born in England
He's an Indian man
If a Chinese man born in Scotland
He's a Chinese man
So I think it's time
That my black brothers try to understand
No matter where yuh born
Yuh still African[32]

"You feel that's true?" my mother would ask.

---

[31] Ferne Louanne Regis, "The *Dougla* in Trinidad's Consciousness," *History in Action 2*, no. 1 (2011): 1, accessed August 16, 2015, http://uwispace.sta.uwi.edu/dspace/bitstream/handle/2139/11131/Article%201%20-%20regis.pdf?sequence=1).

[32] Lyrics cited are transcribed from a remake of Brother Superior's classic. See Christine Thomas, "African," *Calypso Music from Trinidad and Tobago: Sing de Chorus and de Roaring 70's*—Special Edition Series (Trinidad: MAJOR & minor Productions, 2013).

"African," by Brother Superior, was released in the 1970s against the backdrop of the Black Power movement, which saw black Trinidadians asserting their rights and reaffirming their cultural heritage. The song and the Black Power movement were both viewed by some as antidotes to feelings of inferiority that had lingered among African-descended people. The song speaks of demonstrating pride in one's heritage by not adopting a foreign (colonial) identity. In some ways, it was the antithesis of a popular speech once given by Dr. Eric Williams, which sought to unify Trinidad's various racial and ethnic groups by forging a strong national identity.

> There can be no Mother India for those whose ancestors came from India…There can be no Mother Africa for those of African origin…There can be no Mother England and no dual loyalties…There can be no Mother China…and there can be no Mother Syria or no Mother Lebanon. A nation, like an individual, can have only one mother. The only Mother we recognise is Mother Trinidad and Tobago, and Mother cannot discriminate between her children.[33]

My mom's family in Diego Martin fiercely debated the song "African." Some family members agreed that, yes, "no matter where yuh born, yuh still African." Others emphatically disagreed with Brother Superior's point of view, stating that they were not African, but Trinidadian.

Decades later, and within the context of the United States, the song still had relevance. As a black person, born and raised in the United States, am I automatically entitled to call myself "African"? What does it mean to say that one is African? For me, "African" is a marker of ethnic identity, and so I probably would not use the term unless it was in some sort of hyphenated form, or unless I was making a very specific political state-

[33] Eric Williams, *History of the People of Trinidad and Tobago* (Port of Spain: PNM Publishing, 1962), 281.

ment. And while I claim African heritage, I am conscious of the fact that I do not face the lived realities of those living on the continent, and for that reason, some Africans would not consider me to be African.

Regardless of how I identify ethnically, racially there is no confusion. Despite the fact that my heritage includes several races, I identify as black; that's how people see me anyway. Unfortunately, being black in this world comes with its share of disadvantages.

The Problem with Being Black

Good hair means curls and waves
Bad hair means you look like a slave
—"I Am Not My Hair," India Arie

Cue: "I Am Not My Hair," India Arie; "Four Women," Nina Simone

I've never not wanted to be black. I won't lie. I've wanted my hair to be just a shade less kinky, so I could wake up, shake, and go. But *being* another race has never crossed my mind. I attribute this to having several dark-skinned women in my family who never appeared to have an inferiority complex based on the color of their skin. In my household, being black was a *good* thing. I remember my mom teaching me at a young age James Brown's instructive call and response.

"Say it loud!" she'd shout emphatically.

And with my whole being I'd respond, "I'm black and I'm proud!"

Arguably the experience of being black is not the same for everyone. Skin color intersects with other markers of identity (sex, gender, body type, hair texture, etc.), and depending on one's background and upbringing, positive messages about blackness may or may not have been instilled. I have met black people for whom being another race has frequently crossed their minds. Although this has not been my experience, I can sympathize with those who wish they were of another race. It's not easy being black. People have made it a problem.

When I started "going natural" while still in college, many people were appalled. This was well (perhaps even a decade) before black women starting going natural *en masse*. I was (and sometimes still am) subjected to veiled insults from family and friends alike about how nice my hair *used to look* before going natural. "Your hair was so pretty and long!" In essence, my beauty is judged on a standard that I can never meet naturally.

It is well known in Trinidad that people who wore dreads could not get jobs in certain institutions, like banks. And throughout the Americas, women of African descent mercilessly straightened their hair so that they would be perceived as "respectable"; their economic livelihood often depended on it. The late sixties and early seventies provided some relief from chemical and heat treatments, but by the time I was born, it seemed like the "Black is Beautiful" movement was slowly fading away. Outside of the Rastas and Afro-centrics, natural was not considered a good look.

For me, going natural was very much a political statement. It was both a silent protest of the status quo and a silent affirmation to myself and others with hair deemed inferior that God makes no imperfections. And would you know, many (but definitely not all) of those who gawked at my decision to go natural would later protest whenever I'd suggest that I might straighten my hair again.

Mi Gente[34]

"¿Y tu agüela, a'onde ejtá?"[35]
—"¿Y tu agüela, a'onde ejtá?," Fortunato Vizcarrondo

"¿Po qué te pone tan brabo, cuando te disen negro bembón, si tiene la boca santa, negro bembón?"[36]
—"Negro bembón," Nicolás Guillén

Cue: "¿Y tu abuela a'onde e'tá?" Luis Carbonell; "Negro bembón," Ismael Rivera

I was perhaps in my mid-twenties when I had a conversation with a Latina that went a little something like this:

"So I met this black guy today. I mean Cuban."

"So you met a black Cuban?" I replied.

"No. I met a Cuban."

"But he's black," I pushed.

"No. He's Cuban. Latinos aren't black."

Race and color are sensitive topics for many people, and the dynamics are particularly interesting within the Latin@

[34] "Mi gente" is a Spanish phrase meaning "my people."

[35] "And your grandmother, where is she?" The question posed is the title of a poem by the Puerto Rican poet, (Fernando) Fortunato Vizcarrondo. The poem highlights how African ancestry is simultaneously devalued and denied by many in Latin America. The question essentially forces those on the receiving end of it to confront their blackness by acknowledging their black grandmother. See Fortunato Vizcarrondo, "¿Y tu agüela, a'onde ejtá?," *Dinga y Mandinga: Poemas*, 3rd ed. (San Juan: Instituto de Cultura Puertorriqueña, 1976).

[36] "Why you get so testy when they call you black and big-lipped, if you have a mouth divine, big-lipped black man?" (My translation). Nicolás Guillén, "Negro bembón," in *Las grandes elegías y otros poemas*, ed. Angel Augier (Caracas: Biblioteca Ayacucho, 1984), 47. The non-standard Spanish spellings in both "¿Y tu agüela a'onde ejtá?" and "Negro bembón" are meant to reflect the pronunciation of Spanish by persons of African descent, and to give value to their culture by honoring their unique speech formations in print.

community, where the separation of race from ethnicity is common. The notion that one cannot be both black *and* Latin@ is still prevalent despite a push for better representation on the part of Afro-Latin@s.

I once attended a formal event where I wore my hair in a loose afro (as opposed to the tight afros popular during the 1970s). My hair flowed up and out from my head, and I have to admit, I looked good. A dark-skinned Dominican[37] sister approached me, her hair long and curly but not as kinky as mine.

"Thank you for wearing your hair like that," she said.

We talked for a little bit longer, and I don't remember her saying much else on the topic of hair. But she knew that I knew what her initial comment was about. She was thanking me for having the courage to wear my hair natural in a space where many people in attendance would have considered that to be an egregious faux pas. She was thanking me for perhaps making it a little bit easier for Latinas like her to embrace themselves more fully without having to succumb to the perm, hot comb, or weave.

I Know Nothing of Collard Greens

I remember the first time I heard the ad for the play *Platanos y Collard Greens*. I'm not sure if it was on one of the Latino stations, like La Mega 97.9 FM, or one of the R&B stations in the city. However, I do remember being *pissed*. The original show debuted in 2003 and was billed as a "hilarious romantic tale which asks if love between Blacks and Latinos can survive."[38] First of all, I know nothing about collard greens and *everything* about plátanos. I may have grown up calling them plantains, but they are the same damn thing. The issue

---

[37] From the Dominican Republic.

[38] "About the Show," *Platanos, Collard Greens, y Callaloo*, Between the Lines Productions, Inc., accessed August 16, 2015, http://www.platanosandcollardgreens.com/about-the-show/.

may seem minor enough to some, and I surely did not lose sleep over the matter, but every time a commercial for the play aired, my fury was renewed.[39]

Honestly, I can't get too mad at the promoters. I have used the phrase "blacks and Latinos" on countless occasions, usually feeling uneasy as I do so. The fact is that, in this country, discourse on race is convoluted, and when people refer to "blacks" they are usually not talking about Latin@s or even West Indians for that matter; they're usually talking about African Americans.

Many Kinds of Black

"African American."

Besides "other," that was the only option for a non-Hispanic person of African descent. Never mind the fact that if I really wanted to, I could (somewhat disingenuously) check white/Caucasian, Native American, and Hispanic. Usually, I check the category labeled "black/African American," but on this demographic report for a college application, "black" was not a category. I was a little irritated. Don't they know that African American is not a racial category but an ethnic one that doesn't apply to all black people? I decided to check "other," and in the space provided wrote "Caribbean American."[40] Let them figure that one out.

Now, there are many people born in the U.S. to West Indian parents who have no problem identifying as "African American." And that's cool; I'm just not one of them. How people self-identify is personal, and the terms they use mean different things to different people in different contexts.

[39] *Platanos y Collard Greens* has expanded to include black people from the Caribbean in a new show titled, *Platanos, Collard Greens, y Callaloo.*

[40] Now, by listing myself as Caribbean American, my racial identity remained ambiguous. This was not purposeful but rather a side effect of my knee-jerk response to the questionnaire.

Furthermore, the way people self-identify may vary over time and space. Racially, I self-identify as black. The racial identity that I project never changes. If nothing else, I do so for convenience. There's no doubt that when people look at me they see a black female. I may have Amerindian and Caucasian genes running through my veins, but in this body, with this skin color and hair texture, people simply don't see that.[41]

However, other aspects of my identity are more malleable. When people ask me where I'm from, I often say, "I was born and raised in New York, but my parents are from Trinidad." Sometimes I simply say, "I'm from New York." Other times, "I'm from Brooklyn." If I'm out of the country, I might say, "I'm from the United States." (But even then, I somewhat arrogantly proclaim that I'm from New York. After all, *everyone* has heard of New York.)

Why do I mention that my parents are from Trinidad? Is it to eschew solidarity with African Americans? No. It's to signify that blackness cannot be reduced solely to the experiences of those who are descendants of Africans brought to the U.S. as slaves. It is a signal not to make any judgments about who you may think I am. As someone born and raised in East Flatbush among West Indians and their children, I am very much aware that the further I travel from my neighborhood the more different I become (even among black people), especially if I leave the East Coast. The further I travel away from spaces where Trinidadians are present, the less people will understand me when I say, "Doh try and *mamaguy*[42] me," or "Gyul, she have some real *tabanca*,"[43] or "Dat FIFA ting is one set ah *bobol, oui!*"[44]

---

[41] Interestingly, I know of a dark-skinned black female who traveled to Haiti and was called white by a little girl, presumably because of her economic stature relative to the people in the area she was visiting. It could also be that "white" was being used as a synonym for "American." That's a topic for another day, but it's something to think about.

[42] Translation: "Don't try to fool me."

[43] Translation: "Girl, she's really depressed from that breakup."

[44] Translation: "That FIFA scandal is full of corruption, yes!"

Most of all, I say that my parents are from Trinidad because I'm proud of my heritage. And no "-ism"—not colonialism, imperialism, or racism—could make me feel otherwise. But I'll admit, sometimes I worry about losing my culture.

Chapter 6:

An Immigrant in My Own Land

"My green seasoning is on point," I said proudly.
"Is that that green thing that looks like baby doo-doo that Mom scoops on meat when she is seasoning?" my younger sister asked.
"It doesn't look like baby toots! But yes, that's it."
"Being first generation is hard."
—Conversation between me and my sister, Dominique

I walked towards the bench situated just inside the front entrance of the Trader Joe's on 72nd Street in Manhattan. As I got closer, an older woman already seated there turned and looked at me. Well, it actually seemed more like she snarled at me. She gave me the one-up and one-down before turning her head and continuing her conversation. I listened to the lilt in her voice as she spoke.

"Trini," I thought to myself.

When she ended her phone conversation, I looked at her and said, "You from Trinidad?"

"Yes," she said with an unexpected smile. "You too?"

"My parents," I responded.

"Although you not born there, you still speak like a Trini. Just the way you asked the question—'*You* from Trinidad?'—the phrasing is Trini. Someone from here would ask you,

'Where are you from?' They wouldn't say, '*You* from Trinidad?' That's a Trini thing."

It made me feel good to hear her say that, especially since I had left the city three years prior, living in Syracuse, NY, for two years before moving to New Orleans, LA. I've been harboring a fear that I'll lose both my New York *and* Trini accents.

Though I had not told her about my own fear, my new friend confided in me that she too was concerned about losing her accent.

"How long have you been here?" I asked, thinking she was likely relatively new to the city with such a heavy accent.

"Thirty-three years," she replied.

I laughed out loud. "I don't think you have anything to worry about," I said.

* * *

For many immigrants, the fear of losing one's identity is real, and language is a crucial part of that identity. While my new friend may have had nothing to be concerned about, I worried that I perhaps did. My conversation with her occurred during one of a half dozen trips to New York that I would make during my first year living in New Orleans. Yet, despite my frequent visits home, I still had an acute fear of losing my ability to talk like a Trini, and with that the loss of some very real social and cultural capital.

My brother and I learned to talk Trini as children; it was like learning to breathe. We simply inhaled the sounds of our environments and then breathed them out. David couldn't even say three until he was maybe five of six. Every time he tried, the word "tree" came tumbling out of his mouth.

"Three, David. *Three*!" I'd tell him.

Nothing like having your kid sister try to teach you English. But he was a child surrounded by Trinidadians and other Caribbean people who frequently silence the *h* in words beginning with a *th* (as in "tree" instead of "three" and "tief" instead of "thief"), or otherwise pronounce the *th* like a *d* (as in "dem" instead of "them").

Between living in New York and growing up in a Trinidadian home, we learned to *code switch*. We'd go back and forth between "Trini" speech and "American" speech with an uncanny fluidity, and that ability would come in handy. During my travels to Trinidad as an adult, I would often talk like a Trini, mostly so that I didn't stand out too much; I tried to blend in with everyone else. As my mom likes to say, "When in Rome, do as the Romans do." However, during the year that Grandpa died, my brother accompanied me to Trinidad, and I often used my "American" voice to talk with him. One day, before leaving the house in Diego Martin to head into "town," Ann asked me a question.

"Ah know you does talk Trini, but David does talk Trini, too?"

I nodded my head in the affirmative. Then she warned, "Don't go talking no set ah Yankee in town."

Being able to talk Trini was viewed as a cloak of protection from those who would seek to take advantage of tourists. However, there have been times when I have strategically used my ability to talk like an American to my advantage.

One day, I was left stranded by the side of the road after a friend of a friend failed to pick me up as planned. I didn't yet have a cell phone and needed to call my family in Diego Martin to figure out my next move. There were a few people nearby with cell phones. It dawned on me that if I asked permission to use a phone with an American accent, someone might extend pity on the poor stranded American tourist. However, if I used a Trini accent, there was a greater potential for some to think that I was being a "Trickidadian." I decided on using my American accent, and the distressed foreigner ploy worked.

But perhaps the most interesting incident that I've had in Trinidad with respect to language occurred one evening when I got in a taxi heading from Port of Spain back to Diego Martin. Upon getting into the taxi, the driver and I greeted each other and made some small talk before he asked me, "Where you been?"

"What do you mean where I been?" I asked, fully knowing the implication of his question.

"Where you been? Yuh sound like yuh been somewhere."

The tone of his voice clearly indicated that he had a problem with what he perceived to be me feigning an American accent. Many Trinidadians take issue with those who emigrate to the States only to return talking like "Yankees" and presumably "forgetting where they came from." Based on my accent, a mix of Trini and Yankee, he had assumed that I was one of "those" Trinis. I had a response for him.

"Well, I'm *from* New York."

"Oh, oh. Okay," he said, a bit surprised but relieved.

Having satisfied him with my response, we had a pleasant conversation for the duration of my ride. But his reaction to me reveals just how important language can be and how a simple change in accent has consequences for returning emigrants.

* * *

I love immigrants. Perhaps it's because I am a child of immigrants, and I grew up in an immigrant community in a city with dozens of immigrant communities. But the life of an immigrant is not easy. It takes a certain amount of courage to uproot oneself and leave behind the security of friends and family to live in a foreign place. This is not merely traveling to a new locale for vacation. For many, especially those who are undocumented, migration means potentially not seeing your homeland for decades, or ever again. Time passes and mothers die. Fathers die. Brothers, sisters, aunts, uncles, and dear friends leave the earth. For some, it is a gamble. For others, migrating is a choice of life or death. My mother always talked about the man who once told her, "I'd rather be poor in this country than in my home country."

Regardless of the reason for migrating, many factors will color the experience that immigrants have in their new home, as well as their relationship to their homeland. Immigrant hopes and dreams are sometimes realized, but just as often they are dashed by the realities of life.

Cue: "Doing Time," Roderick Gordon

Calypsonian Roderick Gordon[1] sang a song titled "Doing Time" during the 2006 Dimanche Gras Calypso Monarch Competition in Trinidad. The song "told the tale of Rhonda," a Trinidadian woman who overstayed her visa and "sacrificed her happiness to stay illegally in Brooklyn."[2] Gordon sings that "she holds two jobs just to pay lawyers fees, and employers do with her as they please."[3] I first heard the song while in attendance at the aforementioned competition. I thought it was an excellent song, whose lyrics appropriately depicted the trials and tribulations of living undocumented in the United States, and which rightly encouraged Trinidadians to think before making that decision. Unlike during the 1960s and 1970s, when jobs for newly arrived immigrants from the Caribbean were easier to acquire, by the 2000s jobs weren't as easy to get. Not only that, but long gone were the days when people could easily get an employer to sponsor them.

However, the song took on new significance when Gordon performed it at the 2006 Dimanche Gras show in Brooklyn, one of the many events that precede the West Indian American Day Parade that occurs every year on Labor Day. In that context, the song seemed inappropriate, as it was likely that some audience members did not need a lecture on the pitfalls of migration because they had indeed been "doing time" in Brooklyn. And although in previous years it was an honorable thing to "go America" (and to an extent it still is), many Trinidadians are now aware of the negative consequences of such a journey, with some even questioning the sanity of those who choose such a life.

---

[1] Gordon also goes by the sobriquet "Chucky," his stage name as a soca artist.

[2] Sean Douglas, "Luta is Kaiso King …Chalkdust Dethroned," *Trinidad and Tobago Newsday*, February 28, 2006, accessed August 16, 2015, http://www.newsday.co.tt/news/0,34903.html.

[3] Sean Douglas, "Luta is TUCO King," *Trinidad and Tobago Newsday*, February 22, 2006, accessed August 16, 2015, http://www.newsday.co.tt/news/print,0,34766.html.

Cue: "Nah Leaving," Denyse Plummer; "Trini 2 De Bone," David Rudder w/Carl Jacobs

One day as I rode in a taxi on my way from Diego Martin to Port of Spain, I heard the male driver and female front-seat passenger talking vehemently about people who migrate abroad. The crux of their conversation was that people were "strupid" to leave Trinidad, only to have to "fight for a living" in the "States" or Canada. In fact, the female passenger knew of someone who had traveled to the "States" only to die from over-exhaustion due to too little sleep and too much work. The sentiments of my taxi companions have been expressed in song, as evident in Denyse Plummer's 2001 calypso, "Nah Leaving." The song, written by Christophe Grant, helped win Plummer the 2001 Calypso Monarch title. In verse two, Plummer makes it clear migrating is not an option for her.

> *Comradery so special like natural instinct*
> *Dey meet you by de river, is come take ah drink*
> *Unspoken but kind, no silent bad mind*
> *So forget New York and all de ole talk*

Throughout the song, Plummer describes unique aspects of life in Trinidad and explains that problems are only natural in a country, but they are not reasons (for her) to leave Trinidad, "so forget New York, and all the ole talk," that is, the constant chatter about leaving. Furthermore, those who do leave are, in Plummer's words, "crazy." The last line of the chorus is very telling. Plummer states that her "navel string so deep and freedom don't come cheap." In other words (unlike those who have migrated), Plummer remains not only mentally, but also corporeally tied to her homeland.

In contrast, many of those who have migrated continue to view themselves as authentically "Trini," even those who have not traveled "home" in decades. For some, distance seems to make them appreciate Trinidad even more, and they do not relinquish their identity. Trinidadian emigrants recognize that there is a purpose for their journey and look forward to the day when they can return home, as evident in a popular version of David Rudder's 2003 hit "Trini 2 De Bone." Performing with David Rudder on the track is Trinidadian Carl Jacob, who sings:

All these years I spent abroad in de cold,
Longing to be home
Trini to de bone, Trini to de bone
Lord, I pray that some sweet day,
I will no longer have to roam
Trini to de bone, Trini to de bone
De problems we have are plain to see
We prove we could stand de scrutiny
All and all, a true democracy
How we vote, is not how we party
There's no place like home some people say
Though some have to leave to make their way
But in their hearts I know their destiny
To come home and big up they country!

* * *

Sometimes I feel like an immigrant and not just of the "second-generation" variety, whose way of life and customs seem odd to the dominant culture. Since moving out of New York, I feel my connection to the place of my birth slipping. And each time I return home to "big up" my home city, the place feels evermore foreign, and not in a good way.

The Hood Ain't the Same

Cue: "The Hood Ain't the Same," Draze; "Inner City Blues," Marvin Gaye

I was visiting home, New York, and taking care of business. Every time I found myself back in the city, I recognized it less and less. Bedford Stuyvesant had been on the gentrification track for probably a decade or more, but the pace with which white faces replaced black and brown ones was rapidly increasing. Rents were sky high; that's partially why I left. Yeah, I'll say it. "The rent is just too damn high!"[4]

I thought East Flatbush wouldn't be touched, at least not for a while, but slowly the signs of gentrification were becoming evident—white people; I saw them. They weren't everywhere. It's not like Bed-Stuy. But once you see a few white folks riding down your block on bikes, or even pass one on the street, you prepare yourself for the inevitable. Remember the subways and how the ride from Flatbush would teem with black and brown faces? Now, some white ones were sprinkled in. And I'm not talking about those white faces that were born and bred in New York City and that would hustle themselves on the numbers 2 and 5 trains past Franklin Avenue to Kings County or Brooklyn College. I recognize those faces. These white faces are different. They scare me, and I wonder if this is the same feeling that white people had when they fled the cities during the 1970s as integration took hold. White people were scared of their property values going down, and rightfully so, since banks automatically reduced the value of property purchased by blacks. Redlining, as the practice is called, was (and is) an illegal extension of Jim Crow laws that continues to persist today.[5]

Forced migration seemingly at the hands of white people—it's a sort of psychological terror that may be built into the DNA of black and brown people the world over. I sometimes think our cells carry the history of displacement. There is a dominant allele that manifests as a heightened sense of fear, like an alarm system shrieking out the presence of danger whenever signs of impending displacement nears. We carry this gene—those of us whose ancestors, shackled, were carried across the ocean in ships. Those of us whose ancestors

---

[4] Phrase popularized by Jimmy McMillan, founder of the New York political party The Rent is Too Damn High.

[5] See Emily Badger, "Redlining: Still a Thing," *The Washington Post*, May 28, 2015, accessed August 16, 2015, http://www.washingtonpost.com/news/wonkblog/wp/2015/05/28/evidence-that-banks-still-deny-black-borrowers-just-as-they-did-50-years-ago/.

were removed from their land by expansion into Africa and Asia. Those of us whose ancestors traveled out of the South to cities like New York, Chicago, and Los Angeles to escape Jim Crow—refugees in the land of their birth, but a land that was never their own. Movement is a natural part of life, but displacement is another matter.

The completion of the renovation of the Kings Theater on Flatbush Avenue may very well accelerate the gentrification process in my neighborhood. Defunct since before I was born, the theater was operational in the 1970s when my parents were newly arrived immigrants. It saddens me to think of the timing of the renovations—just as Brooklyn was becoming the newest hotspot for transplants. Many times as a child, I would travel through Brooklyn and marvel at the architecture of the older buildings that lined the streets. Especially in areas like Brownsville, East New York, and Bushwick, occupied buildings would be interspersed with abandoned ones and vacant lots, signs of the urban decay that was sparked by "white flight" and the subsequent disinvestment in black communities. As a child, I always wanted to take those sad looking buildings and lots and revitalize them, make them pretty again. I thought we deserved something pretty in our neighborhoods. And now we are getting a little bit of pretty. Buildings that stood in disrepair for generations have been conspicuously remodeled, and new buildings have sprouted from vacant lots all across Brooklyn. It's too bad that many of the poor, working-, and middle-class people have been priced out of their neighborhoods.

I left.

Let's face it. New York is a hard place to leave. For all the pollution and the noise, and our unnecessarily rude attitudes, there is a vibrancy to the city that makes you fall in love. But the rising rents have made it difficult even for people with relatively decent salaries to remain in the city. I found myself needing a song to help me process it all, this change; but Mom never sang any songs to prepare me for this. We had songs about traversing the seas to go from Africa to the Caribbean, and then again from the Caribbean to "America," but nothing to prepare me for leaving East Flatbush and New York.[6] Radio has felt somewhat obsolete for years; increasingly redundant playlists just don't speak to me. I generally don't go hunting down "conscious" music on the Internet, but this time I had to. Who's telling the stories that are reflecting the lives of the people?

I found one song and video that particularly resonated with me. It's written and performed by a rapper named "Draze" (Dumisani Maraire Jr.), who interestingly enough is the son of an ethnomusicologist from Zimbabwe. In his song "The Hood Ain't the Same," Draze tackles the issue of gentrification and how it has disrupted the social fabric of black neighborhoods in his hometown of Seattle, as well as black neighborhoods in cities across the United States.

I heard Brooklyn ain't the same and Harlem ain't the same
And all around the world I see the same same thang
Black man in the White House and ain't nothing change
Playing checkers with our lives but I'm seeing through the game

Draze doesn't paint a rosy picture of neighborhoods integrating and benefiting the existing community. Rather, long-standing residents and institutions are being displaced due to "greed, power and privilege," and the "hood" is being destroyed.[7] In New York, it is common knowledge that unscrupulous landlords have been trying to evict long-standing tenants in an effort to replace them with newcomers willing to pay exorbitant rents in a city where housing is scarce. Attempts to "buyout" residents or push them out by raising rents and/or

6 Those early blues artists sang about the "Great Migration," but those songs didn't have the same level of resonance for me.

7 Draze, "The Hood Ain't the Same."

refusing to make repairs in apartments are not uncommon.[8]

Even homeowners are not immune. In places like Harlem and later Bed-Stuy, homeowners have been put in somewhat precarious positions, as brownstones have sold for millions of dollars. Selling makes economic sense for many of them, but not necessarily for their tenants and neighbors, who will likely be unable to afford the increased rents (sometimes as much as five fold) implemented by the new owners. Other homeowners choose not to sell, but want to cash in on the economic boom as well, feeling as though it's a reward for having stuck through the harsher economic times. Why should they keep their rents the same and let these new homeowners reap all the profits? Then there are those homeowners who, as Draze mentions, want to remain in their homes but are finding it difficult.

Used to own our homes
Now we're all renters
Got folks moving south like birds for the winter
They asked mama to sell her home
She said, "No"
But then we had to shake when them property taxes rose
I know you say you ain't the ones in them white sheets
But these suits and ties are similar to me
Don't try to paint me as the black man who's angry
When you gut my community it's hard to build a legacy[9]

Draze not only laments the state of housing in Seattle,

---

8 See John Leland, "For Some Tenants, Only Thing Heating Up is a Temper," *New York Times*, January 7, 2014, accessed on August 16, 2015, http://www.nytimes.com/2014/01/08/nyregion/for-some-tenants-only-thing-heating-up-is-a-temper.html?_r=0; Mireya Navarro, "As New York Landlords Push Buyouts, Renters Resist," *New York Times*, July 9, 2014, accessed on August 16, 2015, http://www.nytimes.com/2014/07/10/nyregion/as-new-york-landlords-push-for-buyouts-tenants-stand-their-ground.html; John Leland, "A Year After Suing Their Landlord, Brooklyn Tenants Still Lack Heat," *New York Times*, January 22, 2015, accessed on August 16, 2015, http://www.nytimes.com/2015/01/25/nyregion/a-year-after-suing-their-landlord-brooklyn-tenants-still-lack-heat.html.

9 Draze, "The Hood Ain't the Same."

but also identifies it as an aspect of racism. And he takes a jab at those who feel that racism is merely the domain of the Ku Klux Klan (KKK), arguing that businessmen (i.e. "suits and ties") that infringe upon black communities in order to make a profit are participating in a system of racism in the United States that has been in place since the end of Reconstruction and the emergence of Jim Crow laws.

Draze makes a point to state that he understands blended communities are to be expected in the United States.

> *Okay. I get it. It's supposed to the melting pot*
> *But am I wrong for wanting to live among my own?*[10]

The artist then goes on to list activities that he happily identifies as part of his neighborhood—dice games, loitering in the park, "[driving] by tooting my horn." And while he doesn't elaborate on how gentrification impacts the ability to continue those activities, I get it. Gentrification often results in black and brown bodies suddenly becoming criminalized for behaviors deemed normal and acceptable (or at the very least harmless) to the community at large: summer fêtes, old men playing dominoes on the sidewalk, salsa playing from a neighborhood store. The most publicized of such cases in New York involved movie director Spike Lee's musician father, on whom the cops were called several times with noise complaints. Spike Lee shared his feelings regarding the well-documented feud, and gentrification as a whole, during a talk at the Pratt Institute in Brooklyn.

> Then comes the motherfuckin' Christopher Columbus Syndrome. You can't discover this! We been here. You just can't come and bogart. There were brothers playing motherfuckin' African drums in Mount Morris Park for 40 years and now they can't do it anymore because the new inhabitants said the drums are loud.

---

[10] Ibid.

> My father's a great jazz musician. He bought a house in nineteen-motherfuckin'-sixty-eight, and the motherfuckin' people moved in last year and called the cops on my father. He's not—he doesn't even play electric bass! It's acoustic! We bought the motherfuckin' house in nineteen-sixty-motherfuckin'-eight and now you call the cops? In 2013? Get the fuck outta here![11]

As Brooklyn has become increasingly gentrified over the past several years, I've been amazed at the confidence with which white people go into predominantly black and brown neighborhoods. There is a confidence to affect change that I don't think we quite have yet. Our experiences have taught us not to expect too much. I'm jealous—not of who they are, but the fact that who they are allows them to walk with a sense of entitlement, as though they have the right to be exactly where they are. Lee has referred to this as the "Christopher Columbus Syndrome." And this sentiment is not exclusive to Lee or New York. In a *Chicago Magazine* article, Jose Lopez, an activist working to thwart gentrification in the Puerto Rican enclave of Humboldt Park in Chicago, described gentrifiers in a similar light.

> The westward expansion of the United States was driven by the idea that pioneers reshaped the land in their image...That idea still drives a lot of newcomers in this area.[12]

The seeming lack of respect for the culture and tradition

---

[11] Joe Coscarelli, "Spike Lee's Amazing Rant Against Gentrification: 'We Been Here!,'" *New York Magazine*, February 25, 2014, accessed August 16, 2015, http://nymag.com/daily/intelligencer/2014/02/spike-lee-amazing-rant-against-gentrification.html.

[12] Elly Fishman, "Jose Lopez's Last Stand," *Chicago Magazine*, October 21, 2014, accessed August 16, 2015, http://www.chicagomag.com/Chicago-Magazine/November-2014/Jose-Lopez-Humboldt-Park/. Article appears in the November 2014 issue of *Chicago* magazine.

of communities is what many long-time residents have been reacting against. And the analogies to Columbus and western pioneers are not without merit; lives and entire cultures have been forever changed, even lost, as a result of the privileging of white bodies over those of darker hues. As Draze explains in an interview about "The Hood Ain't the Same," "At the end of the day we have to co-exist, but we also still have to be different."[13] I would argue that it's not so much that we *have* to be different, but rather we *are* different, and we have the right to be.

Some suggest that gentrification is good for neighborhoods. I would caution against that line of thinking, against putting forth that narrative, for there are plenty of negatives. For one, people who are on fixed incomes, particularly the elderly and disabled, should not have to relocate because people with more money would like to move in, or perhaps more accurately, because developers and landowners are willing to uproot families for profit. To suggest that gentrification is "good" is to ignore its negative effects. I'm reminded of a student who suggested that there were good things that came out of slavery—music and food, for example—which we would not have had otherwise. To illustrate why this line of thinking is problematic, let's consider the old adage "Don't throw the baby out with the bath water." Imagine that the baby was thrown out with the bathwater and someone responded, "It wasn't all that bad. We got rid of the dirty water." That's gentrification.

Economic development is good. You'll be hard pressed to find a person who does not want to have a more economically sound neighborhood that is safe and has good schools, services, and amenities. And integration can be a good thing too, depending on how it is implemented. However, integration should not be a solution to better socio-economic conditions for minorities. Economic advancement should not be dependent on how many white faces live in a neighborhood.

---

[13] "Draze Talks 'Hood Ain't the Same,'" YouTube video, 7:16, posted by "GoJuiceRadio," March 10, 2014, https://www.youtube.com/watch?v=m-khxfDLqp0Q.

Better schools should not be dependent on how many white people live in a neighborhood. In addition, integration should not be a euphemism for "assimilation." It should not require long-standing residents to assimilate to the culture of new residents or vice versa. Integration should be meaningful and beneficial to all parties involved. But true integration cannot take place until discriminatory practices against black and brown bodies—in housing, banking, the school system, and the justice system—are eradicated.

In an interview, Draze makes a poignant remark about gentrification that I think hits at the heart of anyone who has experienced its effects and/or displacement in general.

> For instance in my community, my daughter cannot go to the bakery that I once went to. That matters, because when you're talking about leaving a legacy and passing things [from] one generation to the next, it's important. That's what community is.
>
> You have a people displaced from Africa, if you will, here they are in America and they still cannot plant roots. That's huge. How do you leave a legacy?[14]

I can empathize with Draze, as I often wonder what my legacy will be, what things I'll pass on to my children.

Good Enough

I think about my legacy a lot, to the point that I sometimes have conversations with myself about my ability to pass down significant aspects of my culture.

"Yuh could stew chicken?"

---

[14] Lisa Loving, "'The Hood Ain't the Same': Draze Brings Seattle Together on Gentrification," *The Skanner News*, March 6, 2014, accessed August 16, 2015, http://www.theskanner.com/news/northwest/20909-the-hood-ain-t-the-same-draze-brings-seattle-together-on-gentrification.

"Yeah. I got that down."

"Green seasoning?"

"Yeah. That real simple. Shado beni, thyme, hot pepper, pimento, garlic, vinegar, and maybe one or two other things. Look. I know how to cook. I does cook macaroni pie, saltfish and provisions, accra, peas and rice, pastelle."

"You does make pastelle?"

"I does make it, oui! Banana leaf and all."

"Yuh hand good! Yuh does bake bread and thing?"

"No. I doh bake bread."

"Fry bake and coconut bake?"

"No."

"How 'bout pone? Yuh does make pone, or black cake?"

"No…and no."

I *streups*[15] and tell myself, "Look gyul. You ent a *real* Trini. Go back and cook yuh Yankee food, nuh."

Streups.

* * *

"Being first generation is hard." There is so much truth to my sister's words, although I never felt that way growing up. But as I got older, and especially since I moved out of the city three years ago, I've felt this pressing need to make sure I know enough about my family traditions to leave a rich cultural inheritance for my children.

Some of that culture involves making sure I know how to cook the foods I grew up eating and love. Even though I probably know how to cook more West Indian food than most of my first-generation peers, I find myself searching out recipes to more and more dishes, even ones that my mom doesn't make. That's partly because I can no longer run to the store and get the foods that I want. If I want a currant roll, I have to make it, and so that's what I do now. My relationship to my culture has changed, and so I've had to change as well.

It's not just the food; my relationship to the music has changed, too. Osmosis no longer serves as a method by which

[15] To streups is to suck one's teeth.

I learn the latest big "chunes" from the Caribbean. There are no cars blasting soca or reggae on my New Orleans block. Soca parang doesn't emanate from storefronts during the Christmas season. All I have left are my memories and a concerted effort to stay connected through keeping up with the local media in New York, as well as frequent visits and calls home.

I'm not sure what will happen to East Flatbush or to me, for that matter. But the stories I lived and learned growing up there, they are my lifelines. These stories sustain me day after day, year after year. They are what keep me grounded, reminding me of my humanity in a world that often seems anything but humane.

The only way I know how to keep my culture alive is by telling these stories. And so I've weaved this tale, a few snippets of my life, but ones that I find important enough to be remembered. My story is not unique, but it is personal. It's different from my brother's and my sister's. And though we may share some similarities, it's different from the stories of the countless other first generationers living in this country and abroad. They have their own stories to tell…but perhaps that's the subject of another book.

Cue: "Family," Lord Nelson